World University Library

The World University Library is an international series of books, each of which has been specially commissioned. The authors are leading scientists and scholars from all over the world who, in an age of increasing specialisation, see the need for a broad, up-to-date presentation of their subject. The aim is to provide authoritative introductory books for university students which will be of interest also to the general reader. The series is published in Britain, France, Germany, Holland, Italy, Spain, Sweden and the United States.

Frontispiece Art communicating?

J. L. Aranguren

Human Communication

translated from the Spanish by Frances Partridge

World University Library

McGraw-Hill Book Company
New York Toronto

Library of Congress Catalog Card Number 67-14679
Filmset by BAS Printers Limited, Wallop, Hampshire, England
Printed by Officine Grafiche Arnoldo Mondadori, Verona, Italy

Contents

Part 1
Communication

Part 2
The sociology of communication: the channels employed

Part 3
The sociology of communication: the content

Part 1

Communication

1 Communication as transmission of information to elicit a response

What is the nature of this easily observable event? Communication also means 'giving a share', and is – or was – used in the phrase 'communication of wealth', meaning its socialisation or absorption into some definite group (such as a convent). But here we shall take the word 'communication' in its commoner and more restricted sense of the communication of messages. This is also a form of socialisation, and one that has even been carried to extremes in our own time, as will be seen further on when we come to study the question from the sociological point of view: such extreme attitudes are pejoratively described as 'conformism', or in a good sense as 'adaptation'. There is also socialisation when the communication of the message does not lead to acceptance but to disagreement or even open opposition; because whatever response is given is the result of communication.

Let us therefore define communication as any transmission of information by means of (a) the emission, (b) the conduction and (c) the reception of (d) a message. To avoid confusion, some further details about each of these stages in the process of communicating a message or information must be added here.

First, the process of reception need by no means consist in mere passive 'acceptance', as might be supposed from the usual connotation of the word. Even agreement usually sets an effective process in motion, and it is therefore essential to bear in mind that the word 'reply' always has an active meaning. (This is very clear in expressions like 'give a suitable reply', or 'I gave him the reply he deserved'.)

Secondly, we must fully realise the special characteristics of

A burial scene. Pose and expression suggest grief, but would not necessarily do so to someone ignorant of the context. (Hysterical mirth may produce a similar expression.)

the conductive process – its relative autonomy and ambiguity. If metaphysical theories of direct communication by intuition, sympathy or any other form of immediate contact between the emitter and receptor of a message are set on one side, it follows that the message must always be 'deciphered', or at least 'interpreted', with all the risks of error that such a translation involves. We shall soon see more clearly that the transmission itself is without content, that is to say that there is no meaning inherent in the intermediate conductive process. We must remember also that the receptor need not necessarily be a person, but may be some electronic apparatus, and that the same is strictly true of the emitter. And finally we must make it clear that the word 'message' is to be taken in its usual, everyday sense, without any of the grandiloquence infused into it by literary critics, who by equating it with some word like 'revelation' try to exaggerate the importance of the work they are describing.

The completest method of communication between people is obviously language. Language, as used when two or more people are in communication, is a social event (belonging to the sphere of social psychology). Neither of the two speakers has invented the means of communication he is using, but each has received it from the group or society to which he belongs. Language is thus social in a more exact sense than that implied in its being a simple form of communication between persons: it belongs to society, and must be studied from a sociological point of view, not merely from that of social psychology.

But language as the fullest method of communication, and

its two essential stages – emission and reception – cannot be treated separately from human behaviour on the one hand (of which it forms a part) and the pattern of stimulus-response on the other (of which emission–reception is an example). Under the influence of behaviourism, Gestalt psychology and other kindred trends it is generally recognised today that stimuli and responses do not occur in isolation, but grouped together in patterns or figures. So that there is no need for the study of these phenomena to be purely 'molecular', to use scientific jargon, and reduce language to phonetics and phonemics; it can also be 'molar' or integral, and take structural unities as its starting-point, in our case unities of behaviour concerned with communication. George A. Miller[1] has clearly distinguished the advantages – and disadvantages – of both methods. It is more 'interesting' to begin by analysing the complete social phenomenon of communication, but less austerely 'scientific', especially if it is borne in mind that language is for most people 'a magical and subjective affair' inseparably connected with their thoughts, ideas and feelings. Miller therefore thinks it pedagogically more useful to start by cultivating a detached, impersonal and 'formal' attitude. He is very probably right, but the fundamentally *sociological* nature of the present work inclines us to treat the subject of communication and its most complete form, language, both as a structural whole and a part of behaviour.

Behaviour takes forms that are in part perceptual and in part kinetic: not only do we organise our sensations in a perceptual whole, but we organise our movements in an

ordered series (walking, playing the piano, typing or writing, carrying out other consecutive articulate actions, grasping, cutting something, and so on). Therefore it would seem a good idea to approach our problem by considering language and communication in general within the general framework of organised behaviour. From this point of view, when certain types of spatio-temporal behaviour are co-ordinated with others, with a purpose that is in the widest sense social, they can be considered as true 'conversations' made up of expressions and gestures – leaving on one side the pseudo-problem of the origin of language. In this way George H. Mead[2] showed that when animals – or children or boxers –

Movement and response – a dialogue without words. As in all communication, ambiguity is possible but here delay may be even more dangerous than misunderstanding.

fight, each movement of one of them determines a corresponding movement in the other, a genuine response to it, thus creating a dialogue without words. Every gesture is understood as a *sign*, possessing significance which the adversary must anticipate as quickly as possible while it is still in a rudimentary stage, so as to foresee what will happen when it is complete: a clenched fist proclaims the beginning of the fight, the gesture of making a punch in the stomach may herald a blow in the stomach, but it may also be a feint, designed to lower the guard from the face and leave it open to a blow, and so on. The silent dialogue of a fight is always to some degree ambiguous, like most spoken dialogues. But one must not wait until one's opponent has completed his movement and dealt a real blow, because by then it may already be too late to reply.

This leads us to a second sense of the word 'conversation': each opponent has to put himself in the place of the other so as to decide what to do himself. He must imagine his adversary attacking at one point, or pretending to do so and then really attacking in another, and then try to defend himself adequately at the same time ancitipating his actions. For only by putting himself in his opponent's place can he anticipate him and in due course make a fitting reply. If life is considered as a contest (*agôn*) between two adversaries, it consists solely in this ability to foresee what the other man is going to do and neutralise his attack, at the same time taking unexpected measures to disconcert him.

2 The sign and its meaning

We here have to do with a sort of pre-language (I repeat that I am not going into the problem of the genesis of language, and the prefix must therefore be accepted with suitable reservations), or communication by means of non-verbal *signs*. These signs consist of events or 'referents' ('things') that are physically present and point directly to the past (tracks on the ground, or scent), or to the future (an arrow indicating the way), but invariably to something which has *significance*, that is to say another event, referent, or object.

The above analysis clearly shows the point we have now reached, namely: a) that the sign itself does not transmit any message in the sense of possessing a given 'content', and since it must be interpreted or deciphered a mistake is of course possible (such as taking a feint for the start of a direct blow, or a raised clenched fist for a Communist salutation instead of a threat, and so on); b) that the emission does not always inevitably lead to the simple, quiet and passive reception of the message, but frequently excites an active response; and c) that for the same reason this response may be in opposition to the emission instead of conforming with it.

As we said before, signs may refer to the past (footprints, scents), but their 'meaning' always relates to the future. The scent his dog is following interests a huntsman, not because he is idly curious to know what animal has passed that way, but because by following it he will perhaps get a sight of it and shoot it. Our actions are thus determined by anticipation based on signs of the past, on present attitudes or signals referring directly to the future.

Language, in the strict sense of verbal communication,

Signs: *Right* Tracks refer to past events but their 'meaning' refers to the future. *Below* A Communist salute which, but for the smile, might be taken for a threat. The sign itself does not transmit any message and must be interpreted.

The holes of a telex tape and the raised dots of braille are codes to which a key is needed. Like words, they mean nothing in themselves.

consists like all other forms of communication of the three stages we have already distinguished: emission, transmission and reception. The meaning, sense or content of the communication is present in the first and third of these stages, but not in the second, which is always merely a sign, that is to say something which has to be interpreted and may be misunderstood in the process, or in the case of language itself (no

matter whether speech, writing, formula or telecommunication) takes the form of a *code* or *cipher*, unintelligible to anyone who does not possess the key. To believe that the word *is* the thing (or a part of it), that the name contains the *reality* of its meaning, is – as Ogden and Richards[3] have shown – to lapse into *mentalism*, or a 'magical' belief in an intimate link between the sign and the object referred to.[4] Words, like any other medium of transmission, *mean* nothing in themselves: they are simply instruments which can be used to convey meaning, but which can also support the weight of vague nuances, obscure associations, or confused desires; so that by means of a single word – sometimes given permanence in writing or as the title of a whole book – we seem to take possession of a concept or even a complete theory. Herein, to a large extent, lies the metaphysical *problem*[5] and here also we find the ultimate justification of a rigorous *analysis of language*.

If we remain firmly determined to consider words as mere signs, our original examples of communication without words will serve us as a guide. We have said that there is meaning or significance in the emission and reception but *not* in the transmission – not in the sign or vehicle of communication. After all, what sense or meaning does a blow have? Perhaps none in itself (it may be an involuntary gesture) or perhaps an ambiguous one (the beginning of a genuine blow can be indistinguishable from a feint before an attack in quite another place, or a threatening movement). *Meaning* connotes 'significance', but also 'purpose', 'intention' or 'design'. Obviously such a purpose, intention or design exists only in the emitter of the communication, and in the receptor insofar as he is able to put himself in the emitter's place, assume his role and guess what are his real intentions; it can never be in the transmission, the sign, which clearly contains no intention in itself.

The ingenuity of mentalists who confound word and thing, is derived from a spontaneous reaction that few philosophers

– except perhaps traditionalists, if there are any left – will admit to. However, I believe almost every philosopher would accept Ortega y Gasset's statement that the reality of the table itself is not *inherent* in the concept or word 'table'. But would they all deny that *something* belonging to the table is to be found in the word (and *a posteriori* in the concept) 'table'? It is difficult to free oneself entirely from the mentalist attitude. And what about the reality of pain? Is it inherent in the grimace of pain, as Ortega goes on to say? A consistent theory of signs must not give more significance to natural signs than to artificial ones like words. Nor is mentalism the only danger to be avoided; there is also the irrational attitude of vitalism, according to which what is expressed is immediately present in the expression (the 'metaphysics of expression', the 'cosmic phenomenon of expression', etc.). We shall return to this point when we come to deal with aesthetic communication.

To conceive of a *sign* (of every sign) as a cipher, unintelligible in itself but decodable by means of a key which we must first discover (or at least try to discover, at the risk of error) emphasises the fact that the *information* it gives always refers to the future (sometimes by way of the past) and is therefore *predictive*. The sign has anticipatory value, making it possible to get ahead of events and avoid or modify them. All information is thus prospective, pre-determinative or normative, not of course with certainty, but with a degree of probability defined by the number of alternatives controlling the possible results. This is obvious in such scientific methods of prediction as forecasting, radar, linear programming, automatic translation of languages and so on; it is no less true for science as such, and also for ordinary language, where the communication is continually delimiting, regulating and correcting itself, according to the responses of the recipient and the degree of comprehension of the transmitted message they show.

3 Language and its concepts

It is necessary to distinguish between the descriptive or cognitive and the emotive aspects of language – in other words its functions of representation, and of provoking or modifying behaviour. Or we may follow Bühler[6] and classify its capacities as expressive, deictic, (or demonstrative) and symbolic.

In its expressive dimension language is almost entirely lacking in cognitive significance, but is charged with emotion. Purely expressive linguistic signs – interjections – are almost entirely natural. The language of aesthetics is also predominantly expressive, *what is communicated* being so fused with the *communication* as to form a single entity as it were. To be precise, there is no exact 'message' here to be communicated. The exclamations which 'tell us' most are those inspired by anger, pain or happiness. But pain, as we said before, is not inherent in the cry or the grimace – pain can be simulated or represented by an actor playing a part; aesthetic value on the other hand is inherent in the work of art, but only insofar as I 'see' and 'grasp' it. A work of art loses all power to communicate when all observers with aesthetic sensibility have gone away. And just because the whole message is in the transmission (and not in the emitter) it always has multiple significance. A great work of art is recreated anew whenever someone with aesthetic sensibility contemplates it. Its artistic content is actually inexhaustible.

The demonstrative dimension of language resembles the expressive in its quasi-natural character, but it differs in its concrete precision: just as an arrow or a finger points at an object, it points, from the spatio-temporal standpoint 'I –

…on and transmission: film actors playing their parts (from a magazine …e of the pre-talkie era). *From left to right:* 'Suspicion – the hero …serves the heroine in converse with his rival'; 'Lovers' quarrel – the anger on the hero's face as he confronts the heroine with an incriminating letter'; 'Supplication confronted with disdain – a finished study of strong emotion'; 'The reconciliation – a characteristic pose typifying forgiveness and joy'.

here – now' at what is near or far, the future or the past, 'you' or 'him'. And it follows from what has just been said that a certain 'distance' is established, not present in pure expression. Even the 'I' of the 'am', or the 'here' in which 'I am', gain a certain objectivity from my reference to them. This objectivity already presupposes the beginning of abstract thought: instead of hitting the object I refer to, or at least touching it, I point to it, first with my hand and finally with

the word ‘that’, or some similar phrase. This definitely pragmatic function of language tends today to be considered as the fundamental one. In fact, as will be explained more fully later, language as seen within the frame of behaviour is basically language-activity, hardly more meaningful than other silent forms of behaviour although always used in a significant situation. Thus *action* has primacy over *words*, whose function is to be at the service of action.

From this viewpoint it becomes clear that the symbolical dimension of language tends to be reduced to the demonstrative in the widest sense. Language thus appears to be essentially 'description', an account given to the receptor of things he could not see with his own eyes. 'Speculation' on the other hand, 'intellectual constructions', and the great systems of thought, are sometimes unjustly and with over-simplification considered as pure *verbosity*.

This has led to a relative reaction against an *a priori* approach to language, against attributing 'reality' to universals or (in the contemporary phrase) 'looking above' or 'soaring over things' to their 'concepts', or penetrating inside them as far as their 'essence' or 'substance'. There is no doubt that neo-nominalism is a characteristic of modern thought. Its most discerning exponent is probably C.W. Morris.[7] Morris divides signs into signals and symbols. Signals refer to physical events in the organism itself or its surroundings: for example smoke is a signal of fire, the waving branches of a tree are a signal of wind, the sudden flushing of a face a signal of shame, and so forth. Symbols are signs that are or can be substituted both for the signs and the objects they refer to. Words are symbols, and thus 'fire', 'wind' and 'shame' represent the corresponding objects and their signals, and are as it were signals in the second degree. But, according to Morris, symbols also produce a disposition to respond in a manner that would be suitable to the presence of the object. It is not therefore a question of a simple 'substitution' of the object by its symbol in such a way that the symbol arouses the same response as the object;

the symbol merely creates a predisposition to the response that will be directly provoked by the stimulus. Behaviour may be different in the two cases. The *labels* which according to this theory are substituted for the objects obviously do not possess as much stimulating power as the objects themselves, but they prepare the ground for a corresponding reaction. The rules of semantics relate symbols to the things symbolised, and control the substitution of one symbol by another (synonyms). The rules of syntactics control the relation between symbols (words). And the rules of pragmatics control the relations between symbols and their users, which are of course the most fundamental of all.

What is interesting in this nominalistic classification of a symbol as an immediate experience, acting as a sign of a sign as it were, is the eminently pragmatical sense of such an interpretation of language. The conceptual function is considered as secondary: the important thing is to arrive at a practical definition of language, that is to say to define it according to its use or function. And while avoiding any metaphysical attitude, as we have done from the outset, we are precisely concerned in this study with communication through action, and always with reference to the future.

In this respect, Heidegger and later Wittgenstein brought us closest to our objective. For the Heidegger of *Sein und Zeit* (Being and Time), the primary significance of *Dasein* (existence) is demonstrative. To exist-in-the-world is to live among things, to make use of them, employ them as tools. He sees the whole world as a network of references all having the significance 'for', 'in order that'. There is an active element even in the notion of *Verstehen* (understanding) as expressed in phrases like 'get an understanding of such and such', or 'judicial understanding'. Theoretical knowledge is secondary knowledge, arising only, according to Heidegger, when some failure occurs and prevents our understanding the primary use of the object. For instance, we only begin to think about the construction of a hammer when it comes in two, and the gears of a motor-car engine when they cease engaging and the car we are travelling in breaks down and has to be repaired. 'Speech' is the verbal articulation of this primordial understanding, which, when it loses contact with things themselves and 'looks above' them, degenerates into speaking for speaking's sake or mere verbiage.

Paradoxically enough, although Wittgenstein is much more concerned with language than Heidegger is, his view of it is not so very remote from that expounded in the first chapters of *Sein und Zeit*. Wittgenstein too conceived of language as language-in-the-world, as a form of behaviour comparable to movements of arms, feet or head, in fact as lying within the sphere of general behaviour, itself an element of it. If language is first and foremost a form of activity, of the business of the world, it is easy to understand that its significance lies in its use. Language is not a set of labels but a 'tool-box'. Just as tools can be used for different purposes, so the same word can be used when giving orders, asking questions, entreating, and so forth. It is its use in a given context that gives it its meaning for us, a meaning which therefore defines what must be done in a significant, but ambiguous, situation. Thus language, seen as part of a complete behaviour-sequence, always assumes the character of a diacritic sign.

Our distorted idea of language arises from two interconnected prejudices or misconceptions: one is that in learning a foreign tongue, for example, we previously possess the 'name' we are learning; the other is purely mental and applies to our own language – it is that we already know the thing referred to, even when the 'label' representing it is missing. This would reduce language to a collection of 'tickets', fastened on to objects as it were, and mentally detached at will when we want to refer to them in their absence. These labels or tickets thus come to give names to objects, so that we can talk 'about' them, as if our purpose when we talked were primarily theoretical, as if language were above all a sort of 'symbolic painting' in the 'album' of reality, which was already known to us in a wordless and more or less mentalist way.[8] To speak a language is a form of activity, and therefore – in no grandiloquent sense – a 'way of life' (*Lebensform* rather than *Weltanschauung*).

This is probably the fundamental point of divergence between the current philosophies of today: linguistic philosophy (closely related to linguistics itself) and phenomenology. According to the former, speech determines the semantic horizon of the speaker. According to the latter, linguistic philosophy reduces reality to a lexicon in an objectivist and degrading way, although there is a clear parallel between this and the phenomenalist reduction of reality to patterns of consciousness. For the reasons explained at the beginning of this book, we shall not try to settle this dispute, or even take part in it. We have simply chosen the way that seems most functional and effective.

But the language-game, the game of life, the form of behaviour and life we call speech or practical language may sometimes 'go on holiday' as Wittgenstein so graphically puts it. It is at this point that a new 'use' of language arises, the theoretical; it is the moment at which philosophy begins. Let us read the passage in question:

> It is quite true that, in giving an ostensive definition for instance, we often point to the object named and say the name. And similarly, in giving an ostensive definition, we say the word 'this' while pointing to a thing. And also the word 'this' and a name often occupy the same position in a sentence. But it is precisely characteristic of a name that it is defined by means of the demonstrative expression 'That is N' (or 'That is called N'). But do we also give the definitions: 'That is called "this" or 'This is called "this" '?
>
> This is connected with the conception of naming as, so to speak, an occult process. Naming appears as a *queer* connexion of a word with an object. And you really get such a queer connexion when the philosopher tries to bring out *the* relation between name and thing by staring at an object in front of him and repeating a name or even the word 'this' innumerable times. For philosophical problems arise when language *goes on holiday*. And *here* we may indeed fancy naming to be some remarkable act of mind, as it were a baptism of an object. And we can also say the word 'this' *to* the object, as it were *address* the object as 'this' – a queer use of this word, which doubtless only occurs in doing philosophy.[9]

We are not 'doing philosophy'; we are merely trying to show that from a sociological point of view language is a system of signs or symbols (or a 'game' with rules, as Wittgenstein conceived it), within the general framework of man's behaviour in life and in the world, and that it always relates primarily to some future action, and most commonly to an immediate or imminent future. Linguistic communication, like every other form, always has an anticipatory character, as we have repeated more than once; it looks ahead to future events, as it were. The information that it affords is information through and for action, never primarily 'knowledge for knowledge's sake'. We can reject neo-nominalism, and its way of treating words as tickets or labels; it takes no account of the fusion of theory and practice so characteristic of language, nor of the fact that the primary function of language is understanding-with-a-view-to-action, and that it must be understood through use. The question 'How are you?', conversation about the weather and so on, are words used to bring men closer to each other, and fill an uneasy silence. Equally instructive is the function of words expressing something extremely offensive about the family of the hearer; the speaker usually has no grounds for what he says, but uses them simply as insults – substitutes for throwing a stone at him, as it were.

4 Language as reality and language as a structure

Hitherto we have spoken of language as a *reality*, a part of the actual flow of behaviour (language-events), and also of its semantic and pragmatical dimensions (language as a form of understanding which is in itself action and serves the purpose of action: giving orders, asking questions, communicating desires and fears, and so on).

But following in the footsteps of Heidegger and above all of Wittgenstein, we have seen that we can pause in front of language as before any other object (language-object) and try to discover what it is, and the nature of its *structure* (its morphology, syntax, its significant and relevant phonology). This investigation into language, this form of 'metalanguage', is what used to be called 'grammar' (normative) and tends to be called linguistics today (descriptive and often structuralist).

This *structure* is a 'construction' or 're-construction' of a linguistic 'model' by means of which we can catch, as if in a net, as much as possible of the *reality* of a language whose fluidity cannot be contained. In the past this was attempted normatively by means of the traditional rules of grammar. This resulted also in the construction of 'models' with the didactic character of rules, which limped along behind actual speech, when not attempting to 'pin it down' or crush it into the antiquated corset of classical grammar (based on Latin) and try to turn it into an academic and half-dead language. Think for example of the way certain grammars ignore the present participle ('What are you doing? I'm talking, studying', etc.) or the colloquial forms of the future ('What are you going to do this afternoon, morning?', etc.), all used far more frequently in actual conversation than recognised grammatical forms; or of what the Germans call verbal *Aktionsart* (aspects).

A structural view of language is not in the pejorative sense an abstract one, as is often held, but a scientific attempt to make use of an increasingly close network of linguistic models to capture as much of real speech as is possible and linguistically valuable. A literary and academic approach has led to languages being studied and taught as if they were first and foremost *written languages*, that is to say dead ones. Structural linguistics has reacted against this attitude, attempting to grasp the *phonological structure*, which is often very different from the morphologico-grammatical structure. Remember, for example, the cadence of a spoken language. (Some languages are 'sung' more than others: Spanish, for example, is comparatively unmodulated and even-toned); think of the running together of vocables (enclitic words, *liaisons* in French); think of *stress*. Remember the fact that in speech (de Saussure's *parole*) syllables may be pronounced open or closed, short or long; and that these differences are linguistically *relevant* to communication in some languages but not in others. Remember that although the number of written vowels – a, e, i, o, u – is fixed in our western languages, phonic vowels are not; and the same is true of the phonemes and morphemes of every language.

According to Hjelmslev the concept of 'structure' is the only basis for a scientific study of linguistics. But it by no means follows from this that structuralism can limit itself to the system of 'models' making up a language (de Saussure's *langue*) and ignore the spoken word. On the contrary: although linguistic models are not empirical, they can only be constructed out of the ever-changing, fluid experience of living speech. The tension between speech and language, and the effort required to diminish the distance between them by conceptualising more and more elements of speech and so arriving at an individual language (for instance, a writer's style), are essential to structural linguistics. It is vital for it to approach closer and closer to the *reality* of language-behaviour.

Another concept essential to linguistics is *relevance*. Speakers have their own ways of pronouncing words, derived from regional, social or individual differences. These differences remain outside the threshold of linguistic relevance, and are therefore strictly speaking extra-linguistic. (The 'linguistic spectrum' is different in every language.) But this does not mean that such differences have no relevance whatever: they certainly have when seen from a sociological, psychological or cultural angle. They can even be linguistically relevant if they come to be established as 'models' of generalised pronunciation. And lastly, linguistics can and must collaborate with other equally scientific branches of research. Critics of structural linguistics refuse to see how very close it has come to real speech in comparison with the old rules of grammar which are hardly more than 'humanistic' versions of Latin grammar. Pliancy, continual attentive adjustment of structural models, and readiness to grasp whatever can be grasped and is linguistically relevant in the fluent phenomenon of speech, are all essential ingredients of structuralism. But at the same time it must confine itself to what lies within its field, and remain a 'pure' form of linguistics (unlike philology, which sees language as the means of penetrating a culture, history or literature). This does not prevent interdisciplinary collaboration.

The structure of language as a means of communication is affected by other extremely important factors such as the following: a) Whether the emotive (expressive) meaning or the descriptive (cognitive) is dominant. We shall have more to say on this subject. b) The degree to which behaviour-language uses locutions out of touch with current reality – anachronistic, stereotyped, residual verbalisations, representing a cultural lag or lack of social adjustment between modern and old-fashioned institutions, social groups and forms of behaviour. (The referential theory of definition plays a very useful 'therapeutic' part here, by solving pseudo-problems, extracting the essential meaning from words, and clarifying real situations.) And c) The projection into language of every sort of technique, invention, custom, rule or behaviour-pattern, whose names function as abbreviations or diacritic and selective signs. For instance the form of behaviour called 'marriage' can stand for a religious or civil wedding, or include both.

Next we come to a problem that apparently belongs to linguistics, but really lies outside its scope: namely resistance – which is found for instance in Spain – to structuralism on the grounds that it is not normative, and for other reasons which are not difficult to appreciate. Spanish experts fight for linguistic rules because they are basically concerned with defending the Castilian language against the barbarisms that are invading it, especially in Latin America. This is no doubt a very laudable aim and will lead to an unquestionably useful and important academic control of the language. But the problem can be looked at from another viewpoint – the one we have adopted from the first, of seeing language 'within' the general behaviour-sequence.[10] Language is inseparable from life and its occupations – occupations which at the present day are tending to become more and more scientific and technological. Language and occupations may evolve and keep pace with the civilisation of the period or lag behind it and stagnate. Those nations which *make* history project their language into their occupations, and invent words to suit their actions; and so this defensive attitude in Spain towards the Spanish language is a symptom of decadence. And although a language may defend itself with academic rules, it cannot cure the basic malady – its historical decadence; it is only possible to escape from this by developing linguistically. When, instead of importing science and technology from the United States or other foreign countries, the Spanish-speaking nations direct their own civilisation and invent their own technical instruments and moral customs (in the widest sense of the word 'moral') – when, in short, they emerge from stagnation – they will invent new words instead of having to borrow and hispanicise those of other languages, for better or worse. And as these modern *occupations* spread throughout the population, these technical linguistic inventions will be to some extent absorbed into ordinary language, so that it will cease being 'purist' and become creative and directly impregnated with the modern way of life. For language is the expression of the evolving spirit and mind of man, and the verbalisation of behaviour is a part of it.

The Spanish language presents no intrinsic obstacle to development, as perhaps Arabic does. The difficulty does not lie here but in Spanish *conventions*, orthodoxy, and 'traditionalism', in the lack of help given to education and research, in the post-feudal, financial rather than industrial, protectionist character of our economic enterprises, more and more dominated as they are by investments from abroad: in short in the lack of creative spirit, or – in words more suitable to the plan of this book – in the fact that Spanish language-thought and Spanish behaviour (inseparable one from the other, like the two faces of a coin) have got into a groove.

5 Written language, scientific language and the theory of information

Leaving metaphysical problems on one side, there is no *essential* difference, as we have said, between the various methods of communication: communication without words, ordinary language, written language, formalised language (mathematics, mathematical logic and pure science) and telecommunication. Of all these, spoken language is the *most complete* form. But for this very reason other means of communication may be better adapted to simpler, less equivocal and more exact transmission of messages. We have already referred to pre-language, or silent conversation by gestures (fighting, etc.); here we clearly see language as a system of signs to be interpreted and deciphered in an anticipatory and predictive manner.

Written language manifests, by means of its special code the alphabet, a dimension not possessed by other forms of communication, such as speech, whose clarity is to some extent obscured by mentalism – a survival of 'magic', which presupposes a 'symbolical' correspondence, or supra-rational, intimate and secret connection, between the thing and the word referring to it. *Codification* is essential to communication. The message *is present* both in emitter and receptor, depending on the former's capacity to codify it, verbally at first and later through writing or other technical means, and the latter's to decipher what the emitter is saying. But it is *not present* in the transmission, which consists of signs that are unintelligible without a key. A page of writing in our native tongue speaks to us 'almost' as directly as an interlocutor; a page written in a known foreign language forces us to make a certain effort to translate it; a page of

Below To all except orientalists, this Japanese script seems more like a piece of decoration than a written message. The initials in Roman letters, and the Western punctuation marks, stand out with striking familiarity. *Right* An orientalist is still required, but because the script throughout is familiar it seems to be more intelligible, even though we do not in fact know a word of the language.

激 憤

もうごくな!〃

〃さて、さつきの項目だ。何項目だ?〃

〃十六項目〃学生たちが叫んだ。

〃その通り。ではお前たちの十六人が死ぬんだ。用意はよいか?〃

返答なし。

〃一項目につき一発。さあ、たれが第一陣をうけたまわるのだ? お前だ、そこにいる金髪! 根性のくさつた小ギャングどもを一人のこらずやつつけるのだ!〃

ＡＶＯの将校は三発放つた。学生たちは左右をながめた。一人もたおれていなかつた。おどかしだつたのだ。

ＡＶＯ隊員たちはドアをサッとあけて学生たちをおしだした。通りへほうりだしたとき、一方では別のＡＶＯ隊員たちが窓から催涙ガス弾を怒濤のような群衆の中へなげこんだ。事件の噂は鬼火のように町中につたわつた、ソコイュとその仲間はすでに殺された、ＡＶＯは放送局まえで民衆に機関銃の掃射をくわえつつあるというのだ。放送局のそとがわでは群衆がわめきはじめた、〃ストだ! ストだ!〃 それから—

〃ゲロをやつつたけろ!〃

このころまでにはスターリン像は都心にむかつてひつぱつてゆかれる最中だつた。ネムゼティ・シンハズの近くでコーヒー店から一齊射撃がおこつた。影像をひつぱつている人たちのうちの数名がたおれて、鮮血が街路を彩つた。市街電車が二、三台道路上に防塞代りにされていて、僕たちのトラックをさえぎつたが、群衆は邪魔物をよけて像をひつぱつていつた。

AVO tentang orang banjak jang sedang berkumpul dan ditengah² perundingan itu, AVO mengidjinkannja. Para mahasiswa itu dipersilahkan kesuatu tjorong radio dan djuru bitjara mereka itu menjiarkan tuntutan². Para anggota AVO tersenjum dan mengantarkan mereka dengan sopan keluar dari gedung itu.

Ketika utusan itu tiba didjalanan orang banjak berteriak bahwa mereka tak mendengar suatu apapun melainkan hanja musik populer. Mereka telah ditipu dengan menjiarkan dimuka tjorong radio jang mati. Setelah orang banjak mengerti apa jang terdjadi, mereka mendjadi marah dan berteriak² lalu duapuluh orang mahasiswa berdjalan kembali langsung kegedung itu. Namun sekali ini orang AVO telah siap untuk menghadapi mereka. Mereka mempersilahkan para mahasiswa itu memasuki studio kembali tetapi segera pintu ditutup dibelakang mereka, keduapuluh mahasiswa itu melihat suatu barisan orang AVO jang berpakaian seragam telah ditempatkan didalam studio itu.

Berdiri berbaris! Menghadap kedinding! Kamu semua djangan bergerak sedikitpun".

„Nah sekarang bagaimana dengan tuntutan² itu. Ada berapa semua?"

„Enambelas", kata para mahasiswa itu.

„Baiklah kalau begitu enambelas orang dari kamu akan ditembak mati. Sudahkah kamu siap?"

Tak seorangpun mendjawab.

„Satu peluru untuk tiap² tuntutan. Nah, siapakah jang pertama?"

„Kamu jang berambut putih itu. Saja akan melenjapkan semua bandit² ketjil jang busuk ini!"

Perwira AVO menembak tiga kali. Anak² itu melihat kekiri dan kekanan. Tak ada jang djatuh tertembak, hanja menakut²i.

Orang² AVO itu membuka pintu dan mengusir mereka keluar. Mereka dinjahkan kedjalanan sedang anggota AVO jang lain melemparkan granat gas air dari djendela ketengah² orang banjak jang semangatnja sedang bergelora itu. Kabar tentang kedjadian itu tersebar dikota bagaikan api jang mengamuk. Szokoly dan pengikut²nja telah dibunuh; AVO sedang menewaskan orang dimuka gedung radio itu dengan senapan mesin. Diluar gedung itu orang berseru: „Serbu! Serbu!" Dan kemudian:

„Hantjurkan Gero!"

Pada waktu itu patung Stalin sedang diseret kearah pusat kota. Dekat Nemzeti Szinhaz; suatu deretan tembakan keluar dari suatu rumah makan. Beberapa orang jang menarik patung itu djatuh dan djalanan berlumuran darah. Beberapa bis listrik telah didjadikan suatu rintangan djalan dan menghentikan truk kami, tetapi orang banjak itu menjeret patung itu mengelilingi rintangan.

Diluar kantor persurat kabaran „Szabad Nep" telah berkumpul lagi serombongan orang lain. Seorang jang berdiri diatas sebuah bangku, seorang wanita sedang berteriak² kepada mereka. Saja melompat dari

Roman type seems to 'want' to tell us something, even if we do not understand it; but if it is in Greek, Cyrillic, Hebrew or Arabic, and we do not know these scripts, it remains a completely sealed book to us, and – especially in the case of Hebrew or Arabic – hardly appears to be writing or a message at all, but more like a decoration or ornament, or at most some sort of musical score. In the former case it is semantically – or rather syntactically – aesthetic, not linguistic.

In a written language it is easy to see this double and reciprocal process of codifying on the part of the emitter and decoding on the part of the receptor of which *every* communication consists. We usually reserve the word 'code' for messages secretly transmitted in cipher, but actually it applies also to every spoken language, to writing (with which we are dealing at present), signalling with flags or gestures, deaf-and-dumb language, telegraph, telephone, radio, television and so on. The coded message – which is not strictly speaking the message itself but the vehicle of it – traverses space, whether it is the short distance between two speakers conversing face to face or the vast one between a man-made satellite and the earth, to arrive at the receptor, who *always* has to decipher it. (In the case of speech this process is so spontaneous that it passes unnoticed; but to remind ourselves that it exists, we need only think of a message delivered in a strong foreign accent or with a strange pronunciation, or of words used in an unaccustomed sense, or of others used as abbreviations of a whole theory with which the speaker erroneously assumes us to be familiar.)

The basic code of written language is the *alphabet*, and the secondary code, or 'rules of the game', of every language is found in its grammar, morphology and syntax, as well as its characteristic locutions, ambiguous words, and such phenomena as homonyms and synonyms.

Written language is more exact than speech, although still sufficiently ambiguous; but it is also poorer. This impoverishment arises from: a) the chilling effect of codifying a spoken language in writing; and b) the loss of the positive advantages of ambiguity – its rich reverberations, and the number of different 'levels' of meaning (as, for instance when a warning phrase is said in a friendly tone, or the reverse). Written language tries to overcome this impoverishment in various ways. Poetry, and the language of writers in general, is governed by considerations of style and is most important from the literary point of view. But the same system of signs that makes up a written language provides means of codifying the 'tones of voice' so important in oral communication; exclamation- and question-marks, underlining and inverted commas giving emphasis to particular words when reading, are poor compensation for the natural coldness of the written language. Sometimes underlining and inverted commas perform a different function from the above, and are used to indicate that a new 'channel of communication' is opening: for instance words and phrases in a foreign language or technical jargon can be printed in different type; the reader is warned that he must use another interpretive 'key' to understand them. Many writers, especially speculative ones, use everyday words in a special sense, giving them a new connotation which the reader must discover from the context, after his attention has been alerted to typographical signs.

Although the structuralists of the present day are interested in language almost exclusively as phonology, to be codified in the non-phonetic signs of writing, it is of course just as necessary to distinguish 'structure' from 'reality' in written language as in ordinary speech. By 'structure' we must not merely understand the rules of the game of linguistics (or grammar), but also 'models' provided by the study of literature, style, and on another level analysis of content. The study of literature may be based on a philosophy such as German idealism, or use the 'hermeneutic' method, like Emil Staiger, and inquire into the imaginative faculty, the poetic vision of life, symbolism, systems of images, and the meaning of existence itself as it emerges from all these. Study of style begins with an exact study of the way in which a word's associations, or a rhythm or rhyme, can interpret an attitude to life. And the analysis of content bases itself more austerely still on tabulations of 'word-frequencies' and 'word-patterns' in an attempt to get at the 'ideas' and 'attitudes' pervading the text in question, in accordance with some hypothesis relevant to the investigation.

We see that even written language is a fairly complicated matter, and although the distance between 'reality' and 'structure' is less than in the flow of speech, it is still sufficiently large. So that to further the main purpose of a sociology of communication and try to gain a thorough understanding of ordinary written or spoken language, we must have recourse to simpler and more formal 'models': we find these in scientific and mathematical language, mathematical logic and telecommunication of codified messages.

All these models have a common element: precision – precision which retains only the descriptive or cognitive dimension of the complete communication, except in the case of predominantly emotive communications, which must be treated separately. Only by thus analysing its different functions – more or less formalised on one hand, more or less expressive on the other – can we reconstruct ordinary language as the fullest form and chief means of communication. Once we have done that we shall be in a position to plot the outline of a sociology of communication.

We have known that scientific language, like every other form of communication, is predictive and anticipatory, ever since Comte's *savoir pour prévoir; prévoir pour pourvoir*. For all forms of planning, 'long-range forecasting' etc., the scientific prediction of the probable future, including the distant future, is an immediate object, not merely a means to an end as they are for pure science.[11]

But this attitude is also present in the cognitive dimension of ordinary language: we 'can see what a speaker is driving at' for instance, we 'give way' to a slow speaker, or 'cut in' on him, and a tape-recorder reveals that ordinary conversation is largely made up of unfinished sentences, or 'interruptions' from the other speaker, resulting in a constant overlapping of one set of remarks by the other, so that the conversation runs ahead of itself. And the language of persuasion is also fundamentally prospective, predeterminative and normative, in aiming to modify other people's actions.

The form of anticipation practised by contemporary science is becoming all the time less deterministic and causal and more concerned with probability. This probability is positively expressed in terms of degrees of *frequency*, and negatively, in degrees of *indeterminacy* called entropy (by analogy with the total indeterminacy of thermodynamic entropy). According to the theory of information, this is measured by the logarithm of the number of possible alternatives:[12] that is to say, the probability of a completely determined event is 1 and its degree of indeterminacy – measured by the information available about it – is 0, the logarithm of 1. If there are a great many alternatives, the determinacy of one among them all gives us much more information than would be given by the determinacy of one among only two possibilities.

Indeterminacy may be measured by a decimal – thus indeterminacy of $\frac{1}{10}$ (of one given marble among ten being drawn is called a *decimal digit*, or *dit* for short; but it is more commonly binary, when the code is the simplest possible, with an indeterminacy of $\frac{1}{2}$ (heads or tails), and is called a *binary digit*, or *bit*.[13] Obviously the amount of information we are given in the first case when we are told which is the specified marble, is much greater than in the second case, where the degree of indeterminacy was much less. Information can therefore be described as what is new in state B in relation to a previous state A. The greater the indeterminacy of an event, the more information its complete or partial determinacy gives us.

But it may happen that the alternatives or possibilities do not appear in isolation but are linked one with another in a causal series. This conditioning is *complete* when the conditions are necessary and sufficient to produce the phenomenon that follows, and *partial* when they only serve to diminish its indeterminacy.

Let us illustrate what we are saying by applying it to an ordinary written text. Some languages possess elaborate tables of the probability-frequency of single letters, or combinations of two or three letters, and also of words or combinations of two or three words. According to the laws of probability, every letter and every word communicated to us progressively reduces the scope of what remains to be communicated, in such a way that the final word of an intelligible sentence gives us very slight information, and the last letter of the last word probably gives us none. Since in most cases there is only *one* letter it could be, its probability is at the highest, and its degree of indeterminacy zero.

Let us consider for example, a message transmitted in the Spanish language and beginning with '*Y*' (meaning 'and' in Spanish). The table of frequencies of '*Y*' as a single word gives us a very high degree of probability for this common Spanish conjunction, though less high when it comes at the very beginning of a text, just because it cannot there fulfil its copulative and conjunctive function and serve as a link with what goes before. (This does not prevent many modern stories beginning with the word '*Y*', which is supposed to give the narration more vitality, and set us down at once in the middle of the current of life.) From the table of frequencies for pairs of letters of which the first is 'y', we get the two words '*yo*' ('I') and '*ya*' ('now', 'already'). The text could easily begin with either of these. If neither of them came first we should be given much more information, because only a few Spanish substantives and very few verbs begin with the letter 'y'. But let us suppose that the first letter communicated was a 'T'. There are far more Spanish words beginning with 't' than with 'y', though probably none are so frequent as '*y*' ('and'), '*yo*' ('I') and '*ya*' ('now'). Now if the next letter of the communication should be an 'h', we are informed *eo ipso* that the code or language that is being transmitted to us is not Spanish, since the combination 'th' does not exist in that tongue except for a transcription of the Greek letter 'theta'. And we can now assert with a high degree of probability (and very little information) that the message was codified in English, in which language this pair of letters occurs with very high frequency, and when followed by the letter 'e' makes up the commonest word in the whole language.

The concept of *redundancy* has also a very important part to play in the theory of information, since it expresses the measure of unambiguous predetermination given us by the very structure of the language or other sequence in question. Redundancy seems to become less as languages become more evolved: for example Greek and Latin are much more redundant than English, a language with an abundance of words that can serve either as nouns or verbs, a large number of monosyllables and few prefixes and suffixes.

Redundancy slows up the process of imparting information (for example, after 'enjoym-' the three following letters 'ent' are completely redundant); but it also has its uses, for along with repetition it is the only way of correcting errors of reception produced by what is technically called 'noise'. All channels of information are subject to some degree of noise. Redundancy corrects these errors or helps to do so. For instance, when we receive a telegram, mistakes in common words can easily be put right, because the very structure of the language, the function of each word in its context, and its predetermination through meaning are valuable aids to decodification (though this is always more difficult in the case of a telegram, because an effort has been made to reduce the normal redundancy of the correct message, by suppressing some words necessary to its syntax).

6 Language and games

Every language has to adjust itself to its own rules, hence Wittgenstein's concept of a language-game. To anticipate the meaning of a message, as we have been doing, is to 'play' at understanding what the person we are talking to is about to tell us. This is the point of departure for the mathematical theory of games, in which the given structure and rules of the game predetermine the moves in the game and progressively limit the possible alternatives, the earlier moves conditioning those that follow.

Of course there are games and games. In chess, for example, the rules controlling what the pieces can do and how they move are rigidly fixed. The degree of structural predetermination or redundancy is therefore high, and this is why bad players play their games to the end, while good ones look ahead and foresee the result and often resign or declare the game 'a draw' at an early stage. Again in chess a man shows his true nature: he will either take risks because he is out to win, or play a defensive game and wait for his adversary to make mistakes. Card games are much more flexible, and chance is involved to a much greater extent than in chess – where it controls only which player is black and which white. There is also, in principle, more information about the future, because although chance does not treat the players fairly redundancy is less and the number of alternatives controlling the final result are more contingent, and it is easier to arrive inductively at the psychological rules (always based on probability) governing the style of play of each individual player.

The theory of games applies also to the tragic game of war

The chess-game: the hero plays Death in *The Seventh Seal*. Good chess players end their games more quickly than bad. The high degree of 'redundancy' in chess enables wins or draws to be predicted after a certain number of moves.

(although here the field is much wider and the number of independent and unforeseeable variables that may intervene is therefore very great) as well as to moral and all other conflicts.[14] And those who uselessly prolong a war are bad players, like people who go on with an already lost game. Apart from such variables as the degree of involvement of each nation, and the general belief that for Germany the war

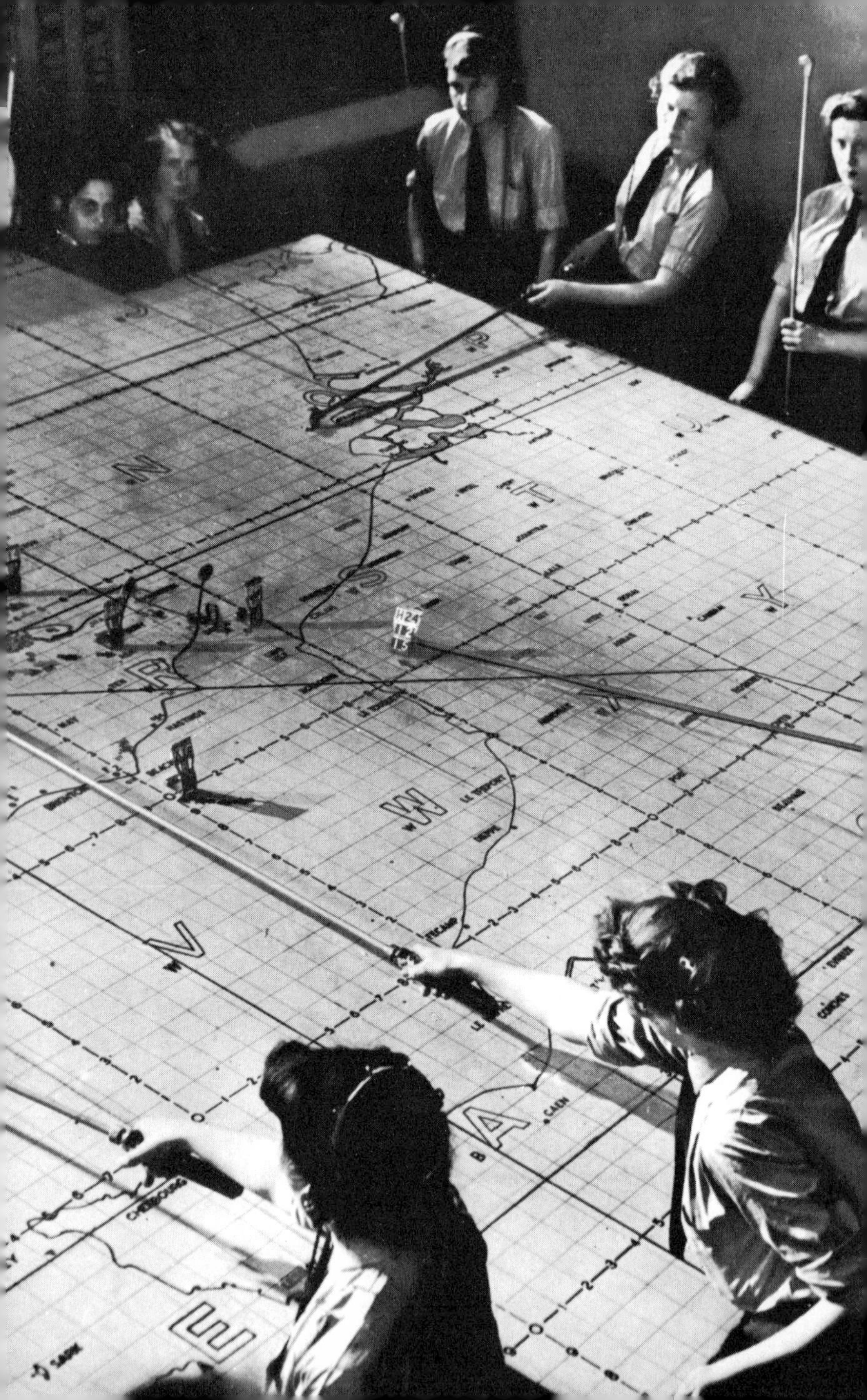
CAEN

The war-game:
air warfare is followed on the grid squares of a map (from the film *Angels One Five*). By stopping earlier, Mussolini showed he knew the war-game better than Hitler.

was a game with no limits thanks to the invention of rockets and the prospect of the atomic bomb, it was not pure chance that made Mussolini, who was capable of somewhat more rational decision than Hitler, ready to surrender before he did, and the King of Italy earlier still.

Not only war, but the whole of life is a 'game'. With love this is very obvious: the cards are dealt at the start – beauty, charm, intelligence, talent, confidence etc. – and strategy appears in the struggle for success, which is conquest of the beloved. Politics is another exciting game, and in spite of the element of chance and the many unforeseeable independent variables which may substantially change the course of events, it is tempting to apply the theory of games to it. I have on two occasions drawn attention to this view of politics as a game; once in a study of Baltasar Gracián's ethics, in which the classical acceptance of the word 'prudence' is by distortion equated with the fundamental virtue of politics, and thus taken as a regulator of pragmatical or efficient behaviour. Prudent knowledge is above all 'knowledge of self' and of one's capacities, in order to judge what to 'undertake' and how deeply to become 'engaged' or compromised. But at the same time as knowing ourselves, we must prevent our adversary in the game knowing us, our strength and our intentions, our style of 'play'. As Gracián says we must 'put our intentions into cipher'. Dissimulation, disguise of the facts, evasion, innuendoes or hints all serve this end; we must increase the confusion by 'knowing how to trifle with the truth'. Gracián was probably the first non-mathematician to believe, like the good seventeenth-century

The love-game: our use of counters
dealt at the start implies a strategy
in winning the desired object.

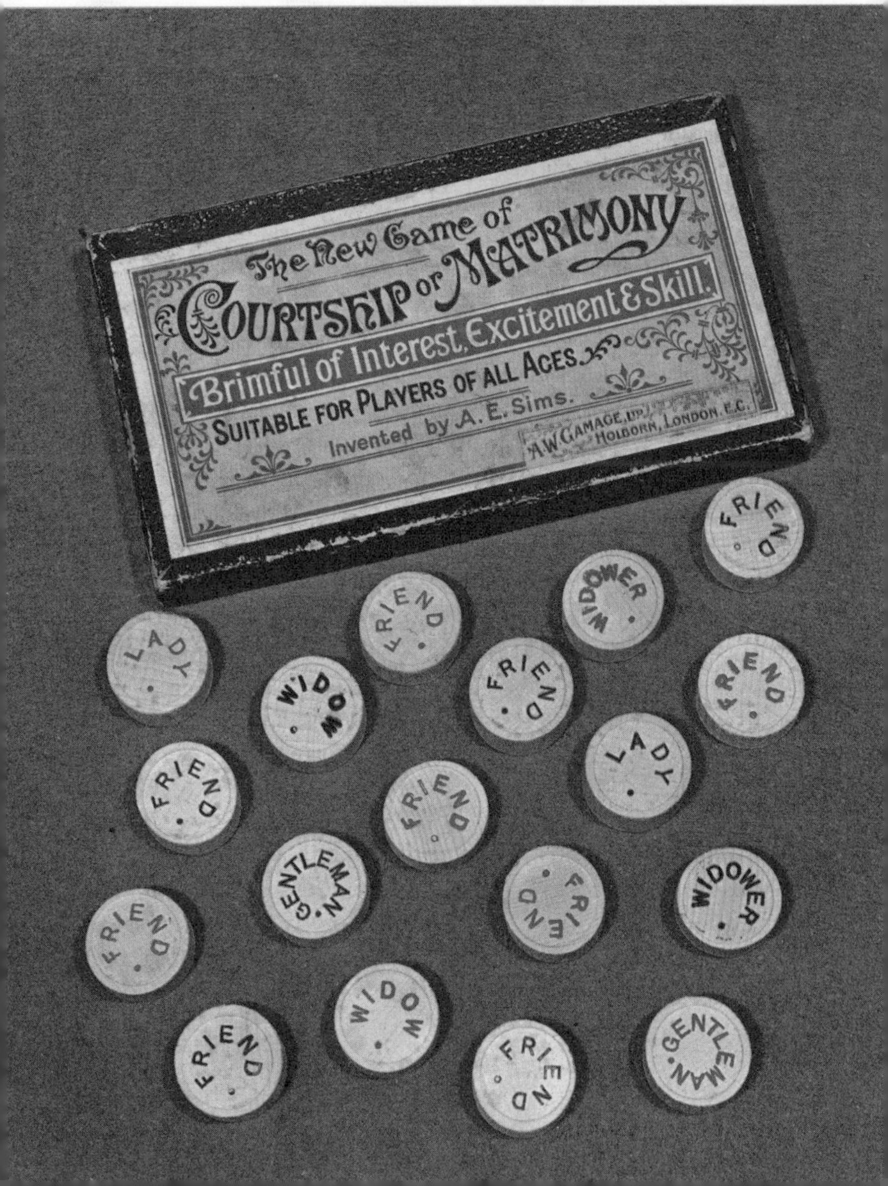

Arcanas rerum ſcrutor Prudentia cauſas,
Præterita ancipiti vultú videóq; futura.

5

The politics-game: 'Prudence', one of the seven virtues drawn by Goltzius – the classic recipe for political success, as put forward by Machiavelli and Gracián in the 16th and 17th centuries. One must know oneself (face in the mirror) but also put one's intentions into code (mask behind the head) to deceive one's opponents. This manipulation of truth now extends to whole ministries of information.

rationalist he was, in the *calculability* of the political game. He was thus a pioneer whose books make enthralling reading.[15]

Gracián conceived of politics in much the same terms as Machiavelli – as a game played by the Prince – and even carried the idea further. Today life has become more communal, and we realise that the style of play of our politicians, however daring, well planned or impressive it may be – like that of Kennedy or De Gaulle – cannot override the facts of social economy and political science. Gracián's 'prudence' has become 'information', backed by a whole Ministry, and generally understood as *manipulation*, by systematically adapting some new items and absolutely suppressing others, with a noticeable disparity between their *real* importance and those it is convenient to give them through the media of mass-communication. The empirical rules to which every concrete political theory must submit are much stricter than is generally believed. An administrator has much less power than people think. In some countries he is forced by the situation (whether he likes it or not is a psychological question which does not concern us here) to play a totalitarian card, followed by a card of concordat with the Church, and then, without abandoning either of the first, a neo-capitalist or a pseudo-technocratic card. The probability of agrarian reform may be almost non-existent, however sincerely the man in power may desire it; but, on the other hand, the probability of diplomatic relations being established with certain countries with exactly opposite ideologies can be increased by disregarding these ideologies and going to the psycho-social limits of absolute practical materialism or amoral opportunism.[16] Some regimes have a deep nostalgic craving for grandeur; others play for inaction, feebly disguised as pseudo-evolution. But in both cases we find a correspondence between the leader's style of play and the aspirations of his supporters. For the winning of the game to depend on staying in power is a symptom of Conservatism and fear of change. The style of play of the leader-player is sociologically determined: every nation has the government it deserves and that its ruling class wants. It is true that there is sometimes a time-lag, because exceptional men act as precursors and are in advance of the actual potentialities of the community they lead. Modern history has given us two great examples: Kennedy and Pope John XXIII. But when men such as these really 'take the lead', or as a Marxist would say take the direction of history, neither the community's inability to follow them nor their own sacrifice is sterile. We see the results of Pope John's desire for an *aggiornamento* of the Church today: he started a process which is irreversible, whether one likes it or not. As for Kennedy, at present we see nothing of the kind. Quite the reverse; but we shall see it – or others will – some day.

7 Communication and degrees of codification

Although the fact is often ignored, spoken language has its own codification into phonemes, morphemes, words, and associations between these primary elements governed by the correct use of the language in question. In spite of or because of its one-sidedness, structural linguistics has shown that the relevant 'model', the significant element in speech, does not consist in perfect reproduction of all sounds, many of which are impossible for a foreigner's larynx to utter and others for his ear to appreciate, while yet others belong to the individual accent or inflexion of the speaker; and therefore that when learning a foreign language, what the student in fact tries to do is reproduce another speech, whose significant or relevant sounds have a more or less conventional mutual correspondence with those of his native tongue.

A second degree of codification is found in ordinary written language, using a system of obvious signs – the alphabet.

Language, whether spoken or written, is full of ambiguities (in a purely descriptive not a pejorative sense), or as Wittgenstein would say of 'traps'. The avoidance of these is the function of a third degree of codification – that of mathematical logic.

Ever since Galileo's day, science has been aware that the book of Nature was written in the language of mathematics. Mathematical logic and mathematics tend to join forces to form a single discipline, the *organon* of all correct thinking.

But modern philosophy has been anything but unanimous in its decision to support formal as against ordinary language. And even if it should do so, it is clear that the latter still preserves its practical value. In any case modern science does not conform to Galileo's too general affirmation, and is already moving away from it: today it is believed that the book of Nature is written in the language of the theory of information. Now the theory of information has been responsible for: the invention of radar; the theory of games; cybernetics (aiming at more or less stable systems for assimilating information and producing auto-modifying, auto-regulating and auto-correcting 'responses'); 'automation' or automatisation;[17] biochemistry (according to which all living things consist of combinations of four nitrogenous bases in sets of three so as to give rise to twenty amino-acids which can be considered as the code or alphabet of life, and which like the letters of a language keep to a structural order and develop in two corresponding series); and for many more results of modern research. Physiology follows the cybernetic 'model', and treats nervous receptors as recipients of information about the environment and different parts of the organism – pressure and temperature for example – which can then be regulated (auto-regulation) while internal conditions are kept constant, that is to say in a negative state of entropy (using the word 'entropy' in its best known sense).[18] Finally, indeterminacy and probability play an important part, as is well known, in the quantum theory.

To return to ordinary language, to which the theory of information is also applicable as we have seen, we find that in its second degree of codification (the written alphabet) it is still too complicated, and contains about thirty letters (according to language) as well as punctuation marks. Transmission by means of such a system of codification falls short of the purpose of language, which as we know (insofar as it is language-for-the-purpose-of-action) is anticipatory, and must therefore be simple and quick. This is the reason why the decimal code has taken the place of the code of written language and the old form of telecommunication – telegraphy by Morse code. But as we have already seen, a binary or dual code in which we only have to do with two signs, is the simplest, quickest and most uniform. This involves codifying, not by letters based on tables of frequency as in the Morse code, but by combinations of letters or words, so that information is imparted with increasing speed. This leaves a perfectly possible role for *prediction* to play, provided that emitter and receptor are subject to the same laws of probability. In this case we use a predictive code to frame an expectation which may sometimes have to be corrected. (It is not implicit in the structural redundancy of language as in shorthand, where one sign may have various meanings and only the context prevents ambiguity.)

When the channel of transmission is very 'noisy', there may be distortion of the corresponding signs. It will therefore be necessary to verify them according to the probabilities of the signal having been correctly received, which becomes more problematic as the connection between the received sign and the emitted sign grows less. The remedy is to lessen the speed of transmission, repeat the emission or use other redundancy procedures. When the signal received is completely independent from the signal emitted, information is non-existent and communication stops entirely.

Here we again find opposition between considerations of

speed and redundancy, with its positive function of correcting errors in emission, or those caused by interference or noise. Whether speed or accuracy of reception is preferred probably depends (apart from temperamental factors, which are psychological and irrelevant to sociology) on which of two different concepts of communal life or life as communication is held – the old or the new. But we must not suppose that slowness or redundancy necessarily increase the accuracy of reception of the message. On the contrary, ordinary language always passes through very 'noisy' channels, and is infested with misunderstandings that slower transmission does not eliminate. (We must remember here what has already been said about individual, racial and regional accents, those due to educational and social differences, male and female voices, etc.). And, as Pascal so clearly realised, if we want to understand a long sentence we must obviously not read it too fast, but it is just as disastrous to read it too slowly and get lost in the windings of its subordinate clauses, and by going astray among the details fail to grasp the meaning of the sentence as a whole.

8 The cognitive and emotive dimensions of language

In the course of our dissection of ordinary language and its elements (the chief object of a sociology of communication), we have so far paid attention only to its cognitive or descriptive aspect. But *all* language, including the most 'coldly' objective and scientific, has an emotive as well as a cognitive dimension: that is to say it transmits an emotional 'significance',[19] (in the widest acceptation of the words 'emotive' and 'emotional'). Sometimes this 'significance' may be a mere 'halo' or 'aura' of agreement, something 'extra' added to the description. The presence of a 'disposition' or the expression of an 'attitude', in conjunction with or based upon the descriptive meaning, may establish an equilibrium between both functions which is destroyed when what we call 'prejudice' weighs down the non-cognitive side. At other times the emotive or expressive aspect may be obviously dominant under a disguise of pseudo-rationalism. In every case of communication, each word, however purely descriptive it sets out to be, carries a certain load of emotion. Such emotions as these (the word is hardly appropriate) may belong among the colder shades of feeling and so pass almost unnoticed. 'Objectivity' usually implies 'distance', or in emotional terms 'impartiality' or 'indifference'. On the other hand interjections or communications with emotional significance (often not even verbalised, like tears and laughter) clearly show the primacy of the emotive dimension. But it must be understood that both these expressions – 'the emotive dimension' and the 'cognitive dimension' – are 'structural models', or as they used to be called 'ideal types', and not a part of real language or communication, which always consists (in different degrees according to type) of a descriptive significance with an affective concomitant, or – conversely – of a verbalised emotive 'significance'. This is to some degree rationalised even in the case of interjections, or at least given 'intention'. The study of purely non-verbal communication belongs of course to psychology and does not concern us here,[20] but it does interest us enormously when it is associated with some verbalisation, however rudimentary.

The analysis of the emotive or expressive dimension of communication only concerns us here insofar as it is a part of a behaviour-language series, even if this is only minimally apparent as a system of purely diacritic signs. Several different types of emotive reference must be distinguished: 1. musical semantics; 2. semantics of the plastic arts; 3. semantics of religion; 4. language as language-game (not in Wittgenstein's sense of the 'rules of the linguistic game' referred to above) that is to say as finality without end to use Kantian language, as language without utilitarian function. True play upon words, or talking for talking's sake, and poetry – to the extent that, as Mallarmé said, a poem is not made up of ideas but of pure words – belong to this class of emotive language, which reaches its culmination when it is applied to the game of life and puts emotions and attitudes into words – the language of love, of giving orders, of entreaty and so on. All these uses, which would have to be analysed separately if this were a treatise on logic, can here be grouped together within the semantics of poetry and literature in general; 5. semantics of theology and metaphysics.

It will be noticed that this classification depends on their degree of verbalisation. We will go on to examine each of these forms of communication in turn. The factor they all have in common as primarily emotive forms of expression (though this is doubtful in the case of theology and metaphysics) is that what is communicated appears to be fused with the communication itself to make a single entity; that is to say that the communication in every case *is* – consists of – what is communicated, and there is no need to refer to 'misunderstanding' or 'noise' in the emission. If misunderstanding and interference exist they form part of the communication. (This somewhat too categorical statement will be qualified later, but has been used, even at the risk of oversimplification, to emphasise – or even exaggerate – the difference between descriptive semantics and the semantics we have called emotive.)

9 Non-linguistic communication: music and the plastic arts

We must stress the likeness to a *game* of all art, not as the word has been used earlier in this book – as a struggle, subjected to rules – but in the more 'playful' sense suggested in the last section, which is in no way incompatible with tragedy. Art, like children's play, is free from constraint and particularly from bondage to what is somewhat hastily called 'reality'.

In contrast to communication through language, non-linguistic communication (and particularly music with its non-figurative symbolism) gives less importance to the de-notative dimension, the semiotic reference to a *denotatum* or thing. This function disappears in music and the non-figurative plastic arts, and gives way in the figurative plastic arts to a purely presentational semantics of what is really 'inexpressible'. In artistic-literary communication (following the descending scale: music – plastic arts – poetry – literature) the receptor retains considerable freedom from the emitter in decoding the message; or, as we said before, what is communicated *is* the communication itself, what is emitted is what is received. In other words: a work of art, as we have noted, exists only insofar as it is perceived – whether by a very small élite, a minority or the general public. And for the same reason it is susceptible of being decoded and interpreted in completely different ways. The greatest works of art remain available to men of every generation. Hence the inexhaustible richness of art.

To take music first, we must ask ourselves whether, in view of this 'freedom' on the part of the receptor, no 'musical language' exists. Evidently it does, in the form of musical

Two musical codes:
Above The opening of Prelude 7 from Part II of Bach's *Well-tempered Clavier*.
Below A page of the score of Stockhausen's *Studie II*.

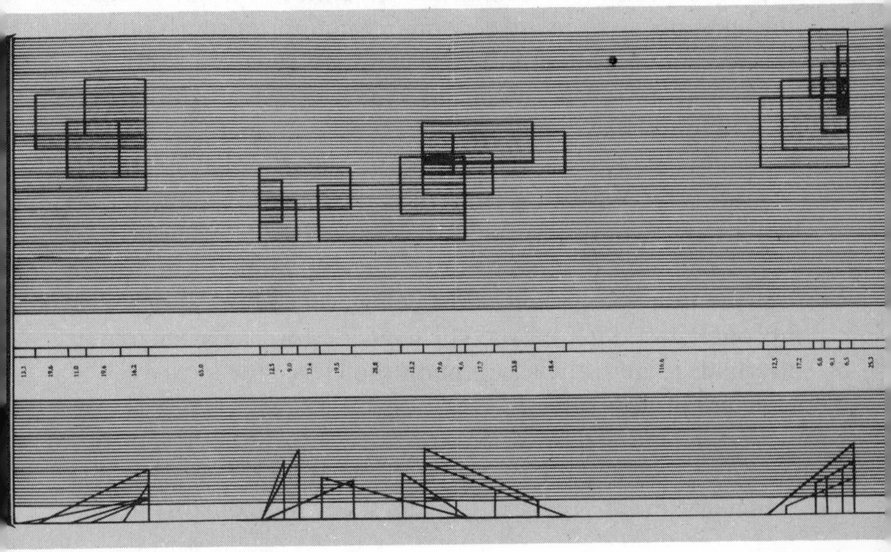

notation, which stands in a corresponding relation to music itself as writing does to ordinary speech. There is therefore a 'musical code', which interpreter or performer has to decipher, just as he might translate a foreign language or decode a telecommunicated message. But is this musical code purely syntactic – the distortions produced by the twelve-tone scale, for instance, being analogous to those of 'pure poetry' – or is it also semantic, or at least capable of becoming so? The frequent and primitive association of all forms of music with singing, its not uncommon ritual function, its rhythm (associated with dancing or possibly with work), all seem to point to some form of cult or ritual as the origin of musical semantics, or at least as contributing to its 'meaning'.

But the form of secular music known as 'programme music' either has recourse to onomatopoeia and portrays or imitates natural sounds from bird-song to storm, or interprets and expresses emotions, thus showing a purpose, especially an emotional purpose (expression of and arousal of special states of mind).[21] Sometimes, too, music expresses 'vulgar' or 'aesthetic' emotions, far removed from the 'natural' reactions of pain, compassion, happiness and so on.[22]

In his *Dehumanisation of Art*,[23] Ortega was influenced by a morphological view of art. His contribution to the sociology of art starts from the assumption that some art is incomprehensible to the 'masses' (Debussy for example), because human beings are divided into 'those who understand and those who do not understand' (and who never will be able to understand). We shall return soon to this aristocratic appraisal of the human spirit, in connection with the theory of communication. This is not true however: Debussy and the corresponding painters of his day – the impressionists – are enjoyed by all sorts of people today . . . except modern artists. What is probably most astonishing about Ortega's essay is not the combination of errors – which (in spite of his acuteness and perspicacity) are noticeable in it *today* (though not at the time he was writing) – but his chief error, which arises out of the very *sociological attitude* he was so anxious to adopt: his view that contemporary art 'lacks transcendency'. 'This does not mean', he writes, 'that art is less important to the average man of today than it was to the men of yesterday, but rather that the artist himself sees his work as untranscendent. But even this does not exactly describe the true situation. Because the fact is – not that the artist finds his work and profession uninteresting, but that it interests him for the precise reason that it is without serious importance, and in proportion to that lack.'

It seems to me that in this passage, and in all his criticisms, Ortega confuses two things: the lack of transcendency of the epoch in which he was writing – a frivolous, pleasure-seeking period between two world wars (or to be more exact between the end of the first and the advent of Hitlerism) and the 'lack of transcendency of art'. *Today* (once more I emphasise the word) the first of the two is obvious to us. But just because it was a frivolous age its art could not reflect it – nor predict it, for even the present is predictable – except by cutting capers (*pirueteo universal*), as Ortega describes it on the same page. When, some years later, events took a dramatic turn,

art remained as *unconventional* as before, yet at the same time engaged, *formal*, serious, human and not without feeling. Non-figurative art is very far from being a synonym for dehumanisation.

With this concluding remark, we enter the field of the plastic arts. Even when these are figurative, they do not uselessly copy or duplicate reality, but always to some extent 'formalise' or interpret it in aesthetic terms of perspective, light, air, expression and so on. Although the artist as we

Francis Picabia: *Conversation.*
A painting of the 1920's.

have seen emits an essentially ambiguous message capable of being decoded in many different ways, he is the prophet of his age, going ahead of it and moulding the form it takes. This, rather than any innate 'lack of popular appeal', is the reason why art is hard to understand. And it is also the very reason why we should try to overcome our failure to understand, instead of falling into facile assumptions about an 'aesthetic sense' belonging to the privileged few.[24]

I have always disagreed with art critics in believing that those who are unaccustomed to modern art are justified in greeting examples of it with the phrase 'I don't understand it'. Man is 'in communication' with any object that has meaning for him. When a visitor to an exhibition says 'I don't understand', his attitude differs very little from that of someone talking on the telephone when he thinks he has been cut off. 'I can't hear', 'speak up', he says, or something of the sort. Or when someone gets into a lift, presses the button and finds that nothing happens; it is not working. All three examples show awareness that the system of emissions and receptions which make up communication has been cut off. The visitor to the exhibition of modern art has entered 'hoping' to find 'beautiful' works there, in the usual sense of the word 'beauty': representations of the real world of the senses, in the established tradition of select, conformist 'patterns'. This system of patterns is a real linguistic–aesthetic code, available to everyone of average culture. Our hypothetical visitor soon finds that his 'key' is no use to him: the exhibits have not the remotest likeness to the figurative painting or sculpture belonging to his system of expectations.

Constantin Brancusi: *Princess X.* It 'represents' nothing but 'communicates' a great deal.

So that his exclamation 'I don't understand it!' is perfectly justified. But he must try to understand; communication must be re-established. There is no need of a new 'key', as the well-meaning visitor often supposes. Rather is it a question of 'interference'.

Abstract art, as it is called, does lay claim to a 'key' however: it does not present us with reality, but with its archetype, its ideal 'geometry', its pure form. Abstract art, the art of pure form, might be said to accord with a philosophy of ideal prototypes. But after the art that is sternly described as abstract we find nothing of the sort. Some observers are aware of the vital impulse, the power of expression when liberated from form, the solid reality of great works of modern art; certainly they 'represent' nothing but they 'communicate' a great deal, even if in a 'formless' manner, that is to say expressive rather than discursive.

We were saying that an exhibition of non-figurative art raises the problem of 'communication', and that the difficulties experienced came from 'interference'. This must be elucidated. Modern science, as we have seen, tends to organise itself and our relation to things in the form of a general theory of information. What is important therefore is that the message should be intelligible, and contain a meaning that can be grasped. Ordinary art, art that is trivially figurative, fulfils this condition in much the same manner as a telephone or lift in working order. But living art shows us the other face of reality; not in an enigmatic manner decipherable with the aid of a 'key'. No, to understand modern art we must have done with 'keys', which are themselves producers

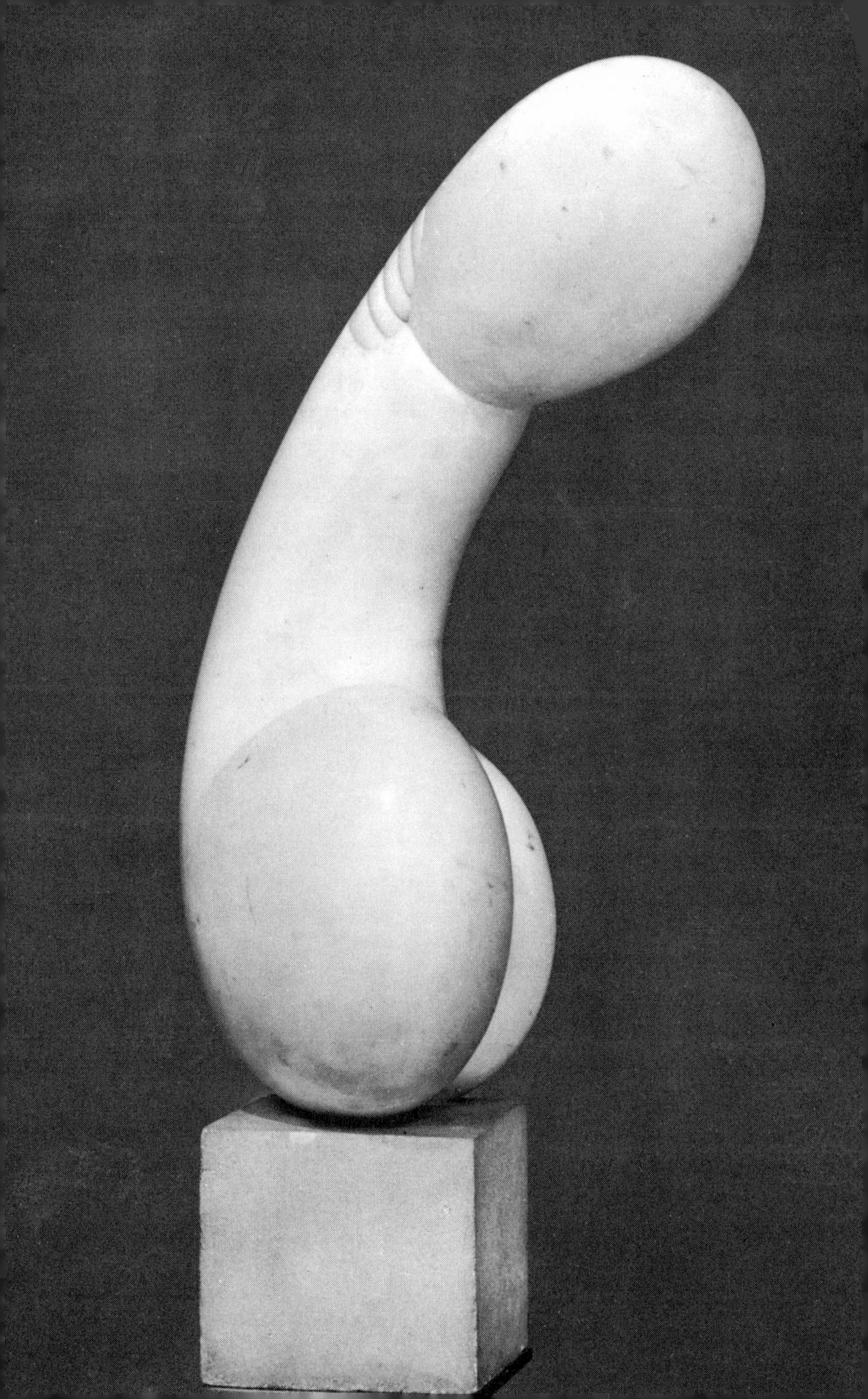

of ‘interference’. If as we entered the exhibition we had left at the door our aesthetic preconceptions, conventional ideas of beauty, and rational hopes that art would teach us about or represent things, we should have been better prepared to be impressed by these works, and that ‘supercommunication’ would have been established between them and us in which the authentic aesthetic experience consists. Interference would have been suppressed, and man would see himself and his destiny through the medium of these works of art.

10 The semantics of religion

Religion is not, as there was a tendency to believe throughout the nineteenth century, a derivative phenomenon (rooted in animism, magic and totemism).[25] Nor is it founded on delusion. It is the highest example of that antepredicative affirmation whose different forms have been painstakingly and subtly analysed by Merleau-Ponty. The semantics of what is sacred has its own syntax. An inner sense of the presence of the Deity, veneration of his power, the need for prayer, and intense devotion combine to create the religious attitude of mind. If we return once more to the notion of a 'game' (but a playful one not an *agon* or struggle) in which all races and all men take part, particularly in childhood, we shall find that one of its aspects – the third – is the establishment of the 'ritual', or rules of the game. The practice of religion is a game played before the Deity. This is why one of the essential ingredients of the religious *attitude* is *ritual* – the establishment of gestures of worship and ceremonial in which religious observance consists. Lévi-Strauss drew attention, in *La Pensée Sauvage*, this close link between ritual and games. But if we understand a game exclusively in the sense of an *agon* (in a more or less playful sense) between two adversaries, we are forced to conclude that a ritual is nothing but a conventionalised ceremonial game, whose 'result' is as predictable as each 'move'. Now in one sense the function of games as *play* comes before their *agonistic* function, and definitely springs from the same spiritual source to which Emil Staiger referred when speaking of the poet's imagination. The poet too is a child at play, whether his play is as untranscendent as modern art was to Ortega, or on the contrary a transcendent game. And when civilised man carries out a ceremony, he is taking part in a game which is to him supremely transcendent.

Magic was believed to have been the 'origin' of religion by some of those who, in the last century, found it necessary to go right back to the pseudo-problem of the 'origins' of everything. But this is far from being the case, as has been clearly seen by Susanne K. Langer,[26] who agreed with Vierkandt that it was only the 'effect' which completed the ritual. She quotes the example of rain-making rituals. To think that such a rite is primarily a technique (magic) for producing rain is to project nineteenth-century utilitarianism into the primitive mind; it is an instance of rationalist blindness to religious phenomena, whether they are believed in or not. As Susanne Langer writes, a savage

> dances *with* the rain, he invites the elements to do their part, as they are thought to be somewhere about and merely irresponsive. This accounts for the fact that no evidence of past failures discourages his practices; for if heaven and earth do not answer him, the rite is simply unconsummated; it was not therefore a 'mistake'. Its failure can be redeemed by finding some extenuating circumstance, some 'counter-charm' that explains the miscarriage of the usual climax.

Rituals are not magic because they are not primarily practical or utilitarian, but religious. Another example from Catholicism confirms the previous interpretation: Mass and Eucharist are mystical representations of Christ's sacrifice, and they prove effective for us and bring us grace insofar as we truly take part. To see Holy Communion as above all a form of spiritual 'medicine' was a counter-reformist reaction against giving the ritual of the eucharistic sacrament its full meaning.

Religion is a mixed form of semantics. Ritual is non-linguistic communication with the Deity. The words of *myths* reveal God, or the gods to us. Myth can also be thought of as a game (stories of marvels)[27] and as legend (fabulous heroes and semi-gods). It is essentially a coherent account of Divinity, and a symbolical narrative of cosmic scope and epic character, unrelated to history. The transition from the mythical to the historical religions (Jewish – Christian) may be expressed by a play on words as that from *story* to *history* – to those events, or series of unique, real, historical events, on which our Western religion is founded.[28]

Are we, as Susanne Langer seems to think, doomed to let the semantics of myth and religion disappear, in order to look at reality in the modern manner – scientifically, empirically and rationally, with almost a mania for 'data' and 'facts', and an unprecedented interest in new systems of information? Must science necessarily triumph, and are we destined to understand the whole universe in terms of cybernetics,[29] at least until, having reached the limit of rational thought and its way of confronting reality, we begin to seek some new mythology, some new form of religion? But have not some clear-sighted observers of our epoch (Roland Barthes, Edgar Morin and Gillo Dorfles, for example) written about new, profane 'mythologies' as appropriate to the present day as the austerity of contemporary science?

11 Mixed semantics: theology, poetry and the problem of metaphysics

If we accept the semantic value of religion and the validity of the revealed 'truths' of historical religions, it is clearly perfectly reasonable to try and 'synthesise' these facts in a theological *argument* (in the double sense of 'coherent train of reasoning' and historical 'discourse') concerning God. Theology of course makes use of reasons – 'it would be highly paradoxical to say that the writings of Augustine and Aquinas (for example) were not "reasoned" '[30] – and even a man as unfavourably disposed to these 'reasons' as Durkheim recognised that 'there is no gulf between the logic of religious thought and the logic of science. Both are composed of the same essential elements, but developed to a different degree and in a different manner'.[31] The best theology resembles the best science in adhering strictly to facts, empirical or 'revealed' respectively, and in 'economy' of reasoning; but it does not claim any closer connection, nor even to be a similar form of intellectual activity. Theology only truly deserves the name if it is penetrated by faith and continually fertilised by it. Theological 'rationalism' was a temptation to other eras, when speculative reasoning without foundation in revelation was used to 'plug the holes', so to speak, in revealed truths; but it is alien to the extremely 'realistic' attitude of modern theologians. Theology replies in the light of faith to the ultimate questions man cannot help asking himself. Do its answers leave him satisfied? Yes and no. They leave saintly and simple minds content, and apparently also those of 'dogmatic' temperament, whose fanaticism is evidence of insecurity (as depth-psychology would soon make clear). If we truly belong to our age, and are neither saints nor fanatics but are to a greater or lesser degree 'condemned by God to be philosophers', as Hegel said, we face the problem and do not try to suppress it as fanatics do. The religious problem (this was no *lapsus*, I really meant to write the word 'religious') of the present day is the problem of de-Christianisation, or to use a more general and basic term, the problem of atheism.[32] I have just called this problem a religious one because, as J. B. Metz lucidly demonstrated,[33] we must consider it as part of a profounder and more fundamental problem, that of the incredulity of believers. It is by means of this that modern Catholic theology bridges over the rift between Lutherans and counter-reformers, which extracts the remnants of the Christian message from the clear and explicit Catholic consciousness. The chief task for oecumenical theology today is to revive and ponder this message in its entirety as far as possible, although no man in any age can live or even think in accordance with the infinite richness of Christianity.

What theology aims to achieve by the light of faith, poetry and philosophy try to do with the help of emotion and reason respectively. But this statement is too sweeping and needs qualifying. Many modern poets would say that they do not write with their emotions, nor even with ideas, but with words. Others, like those of the *Denkenlyrik*, admit to ideas. Meanwhile present-day philosophy is tending to become an analysis of different types of language, in fact to be, in one way or another, a linguistic philosophy; not because it rejects thought and reason, but because it treats them as subjective manifestations, only to be objectively reached and controlled through the observable phenomenon of language. However we notice that, of the two, poetry (rather like modern art in Ortega's view) is reduced to pure morphology of words, almost completely free from syntax and in extreme cases from semantics, or even to a basic psycho-physiological 'infra-language'; while philosophy is reduced to logic.

Nevertheless we all consider the greatest poets to be those who have illumined a new world of their own; thus Abraham A. Moles has spoken of poetry as a 'semi-projective system' – semi-projective not only of the poet's individuality, but also of the age he represents and interprets. This means, as we have already seen in dealing with the plastic arts, that the poetic 'code' is always more or less explicitly semantic, but at the same time by its very nature ambiguous and polysemious, taking words beyond their actual meaning, playing freely with the message, yet never losing touch with the ripples circling outwards from it. There is no single key which will decipher the poetic code; poetry is not a riddle: every reader and every age has their own adjustable key. What is communicated is fused with the act of communication, as we have so often repeated.

When philosophy ceases to be a logic of the different possible languages, and aspires to appear as 'metaphysics', a serious problem presents itself. What is the content of its affirmations? Whence have they been derived? Not from experience, for while it adhers to experience it cannot be metaphysics, and to try to 'extend' experience would in fact be an unjustified extrapolation. Classical and realistic metaphysics deceived itself in claiming to be empirical; although its point of departure was empirical in a rough and ready way, this attitude was quickly abandoned in favour of speculations as subtle as they were purely the constructions of the philosopher's mind. How then did this kind of metaphysics preserve its objectivity? Because it was merely a rationalisation at two removes of the religious message in an impoverished form. This message had first been subjected to the class of rationalisation known as systematic theology; and one step more in the same direction led to metaphysics. At first it was expressly described as the *ancilla theologiae* – the handmaid of theology. This was soon abandoned, but a pre-established harmony was supposed to have united both 'sciences' at the same source. Afterwards an attempt was made to construct a metaphysics on the same plan as the science of the period. Later still, we find German Idealism inspired by mysticism; and, lastly, Heidegger inspired both by poetry (Hölderlin and Rilke) and mysticism.

These messages are very important, but they are not new to those who have been studying the semantics of science, poetry and religion. What then has become of metaphysics? Are its propositions without significance, as the logical positivists averred? No. Metaphysical propositions are full of a significance similar to that of religious propositions; but they are essentially questions which remain unanswered. To return to our theme of linguistic codes, they are like an SOS which receives no reply. It is true that metaphysicians do in fact give answers, and that many of their systems contain more replies than questions. But this is because '*ils n'ignorent pas assez*', and by not knowing how to be ignorant they are false to their own vocation. The dialectics of the spirit is a drama played by three characters: the first, a metaphysician, asks those questions that are of most interest to man; the second, a believer, answers them as best he can; the third, a sceptic, refuses to accept these replies, and not only denies their validity but declares that the questions themselves have no meaning. Whichever of these three we may happen to agree with, and even if the arduous and impassioned discussion between them is often actually a conversation between deaf men, it has more far-reaching significance than any other that takes place between human beings.

We have said that in art what is communicated and the communication are one and the same. In a similar way it is true that what is communicated in metaphysics is a question. Does this mean that metaphysics is impossible? No, only that it is *problematic*. Two comments must be added. It is of the first importance to know what questions to ask and how to ask them: a question, as contemporary philosophers have shown, defines the sphere in which the answer is to be found, even when we do not know what it is. Therefore the science, or whatever one chooses to call it, of asking questions is not to be despised.

Secondly, metaphysics is a part of history, and as such shares its fate. We have already said, perhaps over-emphatically, that we live in an age which tends to understand the universe in terms of cybernetics. Ortega y Gasset spoke of the sins of history. Chance also plays a part in it. In the old days when faith was communal, compact and solid, it was almost impossible to be an atheist. In this positive, scientific and pragmatical age it is almost impossible to be a metaphysician. All the same, whether we like it or not, whether we know it or not, we all are, in a certain sense, and will continue to be metaphysicians.

12 Ordinary language and communication

We have analysed the various forms of communication: from pre-linguistic 'conversations' made up of gestures and expressions; the silent, sacred game of ritual; the semantics of music and the plastic arts; language in its descriptive and expressive dimensions; and we have examined mixed semantics and the formalised language of science and telecommunication.

We have tried, by breaking up ordinary language into its various elements, to understand it better, with particular reference to ordinary speech, from which all other forms of language have been reduced or at least derived. Ordinary language is used in song and poetry; it is necessary to the semantics of music and the plastic arts; we use ordinary language in prayer and entreaty, in giving orders and obeying, and when we conceive of the universe in mythical, religious, theological or metaphysical terms; and by strictly formalising it we create science, mathematics and logic or achieve telecommunication. Spoken language is the completest form of communication, and every other form is embodied in it to a greater or less degree.

It is true that it is ambiguous in comparison to strictly formalised language. But this apparent ambiguity is only the reverse of its richness, its vast possibilities, its ability to communicate information on different levels. For example, a message can be grasped purely and simply on the lowest and most practical level as a request for something. But to someone who knows how to interpret this request in all its complexity, it may be a polite euphemism for an order, or it may be a request for something not really desired as a pretext to begin a conversation about another subject, or the request may have been made to break an embarrassing silence, or be the outcome of a psychological need to talk – or a hundred other things.

Besides, a good receptor will find ordinary language much less ambiguous than it appears at first sight. It is true that some of its terms may be understood in various ways. But the appropriate meaning is defined by the verbal and factual context, of which each word forms part, though taken separately they amount to a pure abstraction and not language at all. Just as we do not grasp individual sensations but perceive sensory unities, or what are broadly described as 'things', we do not hear individual words, much less syllables – but only the statements, questions or requests that are being made with and through them. In the case of a foreign language that we do not know well, or one that our interlocutor speaks badly, or even when both parties are speaking their own language and a phrase has been misheard, we are likely to give special importance to some word we have managed to catch, not so as to isolate it, but on the contrary to treat it (perhaps mistakenly) as a key to what our interlocutor is trying to say. When we are talking to two people at the same time – one who understands our language and all its shades of meaning fully, and the other who only has a basic understanding of it – the latter will decipher the bare practical meaning of our conversation as if it were a telegram, whereas the former will grasp all the nuances of humour, irony, condescension, impatience and amiability that we are codifying by means of our oral emission.

None of this militates against the fact that language refers mainly to the future, and is anticipatory both in the sense of being predictive or prospective – plan-making – and in aiming at modifying the attitudes of other people. Language, as we have seen, is always concerned with action; it is thus inseparable from it, incomprehensible out of its vital context, and always to be understood as part of the general behaviour-sequence.

This primarily 'behaviourist' function of language accounts for the fact that in an age so dominated by pragmatism as our own its decline seems less important. It is a phenomenon that has been remarked on by several writers including myself in connection with the decadence of the verbal expressions of love,[34] and which has been denounced in more general terms by George Steiner in an article entitled 'La retraite du mot'.[35] It is quite true that action is gaining ground from words, and also that the language of mathematics, of the natural and social sciences, and even of history, philosophy, poetry and literature, is tending to become hermetic and therefore impossible to introduce into ordinary speech. In the case of literature, this has resulted in the impoverishment of language and its reduction to a mere statement of behaviour, often presented in the few well-worn words that would be used by the crude and simple characters themselves.

Whether we like it or not, the events of our own epoch affect each one of us, and condition every one of our facilities, including our power to express ourselves. Communication is always a form of language, in the wide sense we have given this word from the first. But in the age of classical humanism, and in the Middle Ages and the Renaissance (which in their different ways modelled themselves upon the former), almost the only form of communication was ordinary language, preferably correct written language. And so if we are living today under the tyranny of a speedy, economical and efficient pragmatism, we must remember that a short time ago we were dominated by literary rhetoric. This is yet another reason why I believed it necessary to analyse the process of communication itself, before embarking on its sociology. The means of communication used by each society give it its own individual physiognomy. And as ordinary language is the means of communication *par excellence*, we have tried to analyse it and the different elements which may dominate in it in this First Part.

Part 2

The sociology of communication: the channels employed

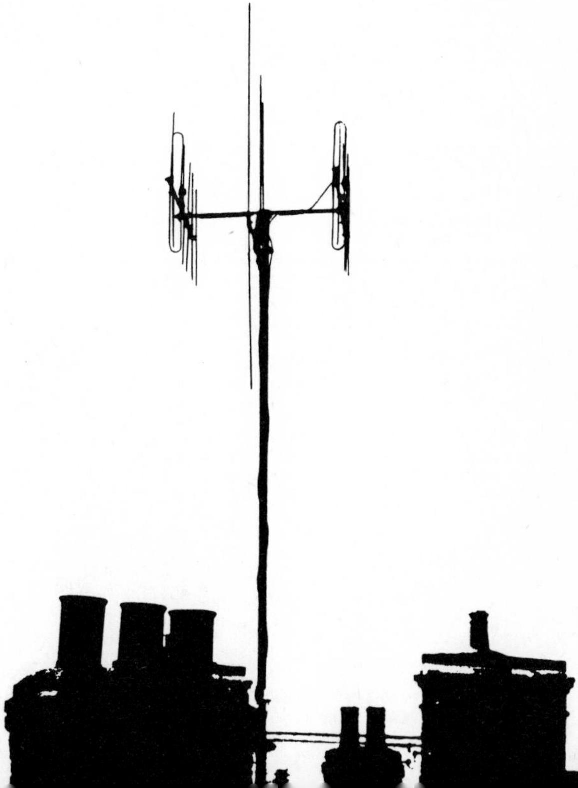

13 Language as a channel of social communication

The word 'channel' is being used here in two senses which might be described as direct and intermediate. In the direct sense, the 'channel' of all linguistic communication is the language used to express it. We have seen how necessary it is to distinguish carefully between emitter, receptor and the medium of communication. Where this medium is language, as in the case we are considering, we must first study it as a channel of social communication. But linguistic communication can take place either 'face-to-face' or not, between two people or in small or large groups, through natural channels (a voice reverberating through the air) or artificial ones (press, radio, television, cinema, or what is today known as mass-communication). Each channel of linguistic communication has a different influence on the receptor, and even on the emitter. (One does not speak in the same way in private and in public, when commenting on a text, or when giving a lecture.) In the present chapter we shall study these different channels of communication from a sociological point of view, and first of all language itself as a channel.

It would be interesting to make a comparative study of different languages and their possibilities as channels of communication in the world of today. Between the so-called dead languages and those of the West, there is surely a third class, rich in literature and ethnologically interesting, but unsuited for the essentially secular, technical and realistic type of communication of the present day. Herein lies a fundamental problem for African and Asian countries, many of them gaining their independence and at the same time trying to establish themselves as industrial communities. Are they to preserve their own language, if they possess a common one? Is bilingualism to be generally accepted where a small and relatively civilised population was under colonialism; or is the language of the old colonists to be imposed as the only possible vehicle for modern culture on a country (there are plenty) which has no national language but is fragmented among a number of primitive dialects? And supposing the first solution to be feasible, should not some of these languages be modernised or at least adapted to Western script? On one hand our Western prejudices lead us to believe that progress and the growth of industrial civilisation are bound to meet with insuperable obstacles when confronted by languages that have not been brought up to date. On the other, we learn from our studies of the subject that Arabic, for example, has great potentialities for expressing completely new concepts, and that as this adaptation progresses, not by academic direction from above but by actual immersion in modern life, the language is forced to respond to realities and new situations in a manner that suits its own structure. Also, the growing importance of formalised scientific language and its ever more complete separation from ordinary language, allows students of different nationalities to understand each other in the 'language' of their special branch of science, more effectively than they could in the days of humanistic and literary culture, when Latin was the universal civilised language. The positive sciences and technology can be expressed in more universal terms than could the older forms of learning, whether religious or traditional, which were inseparable from their original tongue.

What we have just been saying can be expressed in terms of the *ageing* of language. A 'dead language' from this viewpoint does not only mean one that nobody now actually speaks, but one that even if spoken is unsuitable for the communication of what is being said *today*, or that even if suitable in principle, is not now *actually* being used as a vehicle for communication. The problem now suddenly confronting the underdeveloped countries is the same that civilised countries once had to solve, and is still being solved by developing countries where a progressive minority is faced by the passive resistance of the inert masses – a resistance fomented by those who have arrogated power and harnessed tradition to their reactionary interests. But, as we saw earlier, lack of development, cultural inertia and linguistic inertia are always intimately connected – are indeed merely separate facets of the same reality. Languages stagnate when the nations that speak them stagnate, or vice versa. We have no need to know a country itself to find out whether it is evolving or not. From the political point of view we need only analyse what the leaders say in their speeches . . . let alone the *actual* behaviour of these same leaders. From the cultural point of view we need only skim through the books written by its most prominent intellectuals. If the language – that is to say the thought, that is to say the behaviour – shows no signs of new life, the country in question will lag behind. Scholasticism of every sort, a routine approach to educational methods and subjects, the continued existence of the same literary formulas and tireless repetition of the same political topics, are proof that the language and the nation that speaks it have lost the dynamism in which civilisation consists. For it is not a 'state' but a 'process' and cannot stand still.

Nor is that the whole truth; it has to obey a law of progressive acceleration. Beliefs, science, customs and therefore the language expressing them, developed very slowly in the old days; now the process advances at ever increasing speed, words are very quickly worn out, become conventional or topical, and cease to supply new information. It is very easy to tell what generation a person belongs to (and with a young man, how far he has risen in his profession – I am speaking sociologically: of course there are some we cannot pigeon-hole in this way), before we have seen him or know his age, simply by the way he talks, the words he uses, the construction of his sentences, the slowness (periphrases, circumvolutions, padding) or rapidity ('directness') with which he expresses himself. The language of older people tends to transmit messages which can be seen coming a long way off, arrive in leisurely fashion, and have become redundant to a good listener long before the message is finished. On the other hand youthful language – or new language (they are not always the same) is surprising, elliptic and allusive. It tersely transmits a message so condensed and full of unspoken implications that it is difficult for someone who does not belong to the same 'peer-group' to grasp it completely. There are other cases when it is not so much the language that has 'aged' as the linguistic code, the 'key' to the cipher:[36] the old words have been divorced from their usual context and even their accepted meaning, to be put into a completely new situation and given fresh significance.

Physical culture display in Moscow on May Day 1966. A secular rite may serve the interests of political power or the need for a national religion or both.

A sociology of ordinary language as a channel of communication must ask the questions here briefly outlined, and deal with them by its own special methods. On the other hand, ordinary language always incorporates, with whatever degree of distortion and falsification and within the behaviour-sequence to which it belongs, the other 'languages' we considered in Part One: the silent language of gestures and expressions; the language of music, such as national anthems,

Three twentieth-century myths prepared for private consumption by mass audiences. Lindbergh, Garbo and Hemingway, figures whose talents allowed for ready identification with a single large and permanent quality (courage, beauty, masculinity), were over-sold as myths during years of international publicity. As time goes on, popular myths have a shorter and shorter life.

military music, background music (each with its own semantics aimed at arousing patriotism, the belligerent feelings we all have within us, or at creating an 'ambience' suitable to some desired state of mind); the plastic language of art, providing a frame or decoration that may be either impressive or suggestive and intimate; poetry, either as an 'accomplishment' or else standardised, vulgarised and converted into rhetoric; the semantics of religion, used as a personal calmative or 'guarantee of happiness' in the next world, and on the political plane either as an ideological instrument of power or in the cohesive form of 'national religion'. Of course secularised ritual is one of the main ingredients of Fascism. But there are also democratic rituals concerned mainly with protocol – the English parliament gives us examples of these; so do visits by Americans in their shirt-sleeves, no less ritualistic and solemn in their way, to the Independence Hall in Philadelphia, the Monument at Washington, the Jefferson and Lincoln Memorials and the Capitol and the White House in Washington. The secular mythology of the present day has been much studied. Apart from the political myths of Communism and Fascism, and the politico–social myths of the Welfare State, there are others of importance for private consumption by the masses. Among those who have studied these are Roland Barthes,[37] Edgar Morin,[38] Gilbert Durand[39] and Gillo Dorfles[40] – the first critically, the two last attributing real value to such genuine 'mythopoeism', and Morin considering the subject objectively. What emerges from these subtle analyses of modern 'myths' is how short-lived they are – as is also the language in which they are expressed; the promptitude with which they are replaced by others, and the fabulous waste in their consumption.

Finally, ordinary language tends also to be influenced by current fashions in technology and information, and to incorporate terms, expressions and even philosophical ideas inspired, in however confused or simplified fashion, by this new outlook. Admiration for technology has given rise to myths of technocracy, aseptically freed from ideologies; and the thirst for information has produced open or secret distortion in the form of Propaganda. But we shall have to return to these points when we deal with the 'content' of communication.

14 Natural channels of communication in microgroups

The simplest form of communication takes place directly between individuals face to face. Leaving on one side any 'mystique' about the metaphysics of communication, such as we referred to in the first pages of this book, it would be erroneous to suppose that however 'intimate' this type of communication may be, it does not conform to the general patterns of human behaviour. The class of communications we group together under 'friendship', the communication we call 'love', follow channels already opened by the culture, social class and historical period to which they belong, without this affecting their 'originality' or lack of it. Amorous

Amorous communication –
less formal than it once was.

communication passes, or used to pass, through definite formalities: a 'declaration' was made preferably in writing, to give more solemnity to feminine acceptance; next came the formal relation of 'engagement'; careful and inquisitive control of meetings between the lovers – meetings mainly consisting in walks (thus villagers say 'John is walking out with Mary', meaning that they are sweethearts); arrangements for the celebration of the 'wedding', and finally the 'honeymoon'. Obviously all this ritual, which young people of today find too complicated and conventional, is extremely simple in comparison with the communication of love in

Below Communication within secret societies: ritual of the Freemasons (staged scene from a television film). *Right* An artistic clique: Schubert and friends in Vienna in the 1820s.

some other cultures. But this is true – or was true – also of illicit love: as is witnessed by the important and equally standardised part played by the motor-car and telephone (for call-girls) as channels of communication in relations of this sort; we must remember too the function of the procuress or bawd, the importance of certain localities such as bars or 'cabarets', as they were called some years ago – another example of the way language becomes 'old-fashioned' – as 'pick-up' places, or for the relationship to be consummated. Nor must we forget the expression 'set her up in a flat', describing a channel for the love affair that is both settled and discreet and a guarantee of stability for erotic communication; nor the equally expressive phrase (but incomprehensible to modern youth) a 'kept woman'.

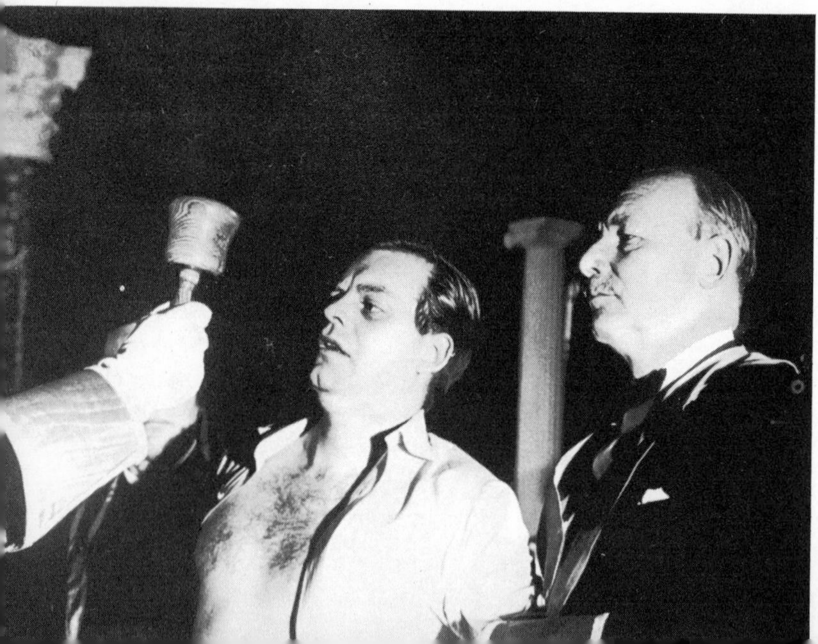

Other channels of communication sustain a relationship between more than two people, for example 'sets' or groups of friends and companions. These are generally closed to anyone who does not belong to the *in-group* or group of reference, among which there is usually a leader whose character determines (or at least facilitates) his privileged position in the channel of communication, as we shall see later. There is also confidential and private communication, and that of secret societies. Both make use of an encoded language, or at least a certain number of key allusions and words which are given more than their normal meaning, reference and implication.

Tea-table gossip used to act as a form of oral publicity, and

the network of channels known as 'parish pump' (communication between women) still exists in the Square or High Street, outside the main churches on holidays, and generally speaking in clubs, social gatherings or any places where people habitually meet together. The most important figure at these is the person who is 'always in the know'. Sometimes the news spreads in less detectable ways; then people say that 'everyone is saying', or that 'a rumour is going around' that something or other has happened.

What has been said of all forms of communication is true

Gossip: the most ancient form of publicity.

of these cases also – they tend to anticipate or try to modify attitudes. This is obvious in the opening stages of a love affair. Friendship and comradeship always contain the same functional ingredient as confidential and secret communications. Admission to membership of a social group is an informal and diminished substitute for primitive 'initiation' ceremonies. And news that modifies attitudes circulates also through more general and wide-open channels of information; people visit an invalid when they hear his illness is serious, they condole with the family if he dies; respectable people stop having anything to do with a woman who, according to all reports, is leading a 'dishonourable' life, and so forth.

Social psychologists have studied these networks of channels of communication and information. Within a given microgroup each member may be in direct communication with all the rest collectively and individually, or he may rarely communicate *directly* with any of them, but often *indirectly* with someone who is in touch with them all. This relation can be kept going by means of such natural channels as 'visits' or 'dates', or through the artificial one of the telephone. Diagrams – in the form of a circle, a chain, a wheel and so on – have been used to illustrate the different types of network. Also the density of traffic each of the channels of the network carries may be quantitatively measured. The arrangement of the network facilitates the existence of a leader (who controls it from the 'exchange', to use the terminology of telephony, that is to say the point through which *all* messages must pass); but this does not apply to the circular diagram. This last system is purely democratic, but not usually the most efficient, though more so than dictatorship by a single emitter, to whom the other members must listen without being able to reply, so that there can be no self-regulation of the group by means of mutual exchange of information.

When a channel of communication is active in two directions, we must distinguish between what are called 'primary' and 'secondary' information. The transmitted message itself is primary information. Secondary information tells us that the message is in circulation and which person or persons have received it. In ordinary conversation the informant realises immediately from his interlocutor's reply whether he already knew the message or not. If, after having run its full course through the network of the microgroup, the message 'returns' to the first informant in a distorted form, this is because the secondary information is acting as a corrective to the errors of transmission, just as we have seen happening with redundancy.

Social psychology also distinguishes between 'instrumental' and 'expressive' or 'consummatory' communication. It is to the interest of the emitter of the former that the message should produce its desired effect, namely 'the receptor's reply'. The latter, on the contrary, simply fulfils a psychological need to express the emitter's own emotions. This last type of communication is not objectively concerned with circulating information, nor yet with creating and maintaining a consensus of opinion.[41]

15 Natural channels of communication in macrogroups

Except in small democratic countries, where public meetings are allowed, the only traditional, regular and natural channel of communication – basically oral and mnemonic – of macrogroups has been the church or temple. The priest in his pulpit was the first of the broadcasters who habitually addressed the general public. In an age of alliance between Throne and Altar, or of absolute monarchy in a country like Spain, the political influence of the pulpit was enormous, and also immune from any sort of competition, since there was no freedom to meet and form societies in Spain before the Revolution of 1868, and the only possible artificial means of general communication, the press, was useless to the illiterate masses. If we add communication resulting from joining in processions, pilgrimages and great religious festivals, and (going further back in time) the primitive 'mysteries' and subsequent religious plays performed on special occasions, as well as communication in microgroups through confession and spiritual direction – if we add to all these elements the authority and ascendancy of the priest over his parishioners and of religious orders, we shall be able to understand the actual state of things during the nineteenth century, and the seemingly paradoxical fact to modern eyes that the nation was Catholic and reactionary and only the more educated among the middle-classes were fighting for liberalism. It was still possible at that time to speak with some justification of 'monastic democracy'.

When man's right to meet and form societies was recognised, things changed. Workers formed into unions and syndicates; class-consciousness and awareness of social rights

The preacher in his pulpit: first of the broadcasters to the macrogroup.

Communication with the microgroup: catechism and confession.

were born; and non-religious and often political gatherings began to be held. These first appeared in Spain at the end of the nineteenth century and reached their peak about the thirties of the present century, to decline afterwards when the radio had become widespread and television had been invented; these gatherings were given an English name in Spanish guise – *mitines*, and represented communication between those who stood 'shoulder to shoulder' rather than

'face to face'. Where parties had formerly consisted of notables, there were now huge gatherings of the 'people' collected to listen to their leader, thus consolidating a means of mass-communication which seems to lead naturally to violence. And it is no accident that this state of things is hardly to be found anywhere except in totalitarian régimes (or those that are residually para-totalitarian) who need these *demonstrations* to prove both to their own nationals and

to foreigners that they have popular support, usually a difficult and expensive business.[42]

From the formal point of view there is an important difference between this direct communication to macrogroups and communication through artificial channels like the press, radio and television. People read the papers when they are alone; the radio and television are listened to or looked at by small groups. Much study has been devoted to the phenomena of emotional contagion during the last few decades by 'group-psychology' as it is called; today there is a tendency for these

Infectious exaltation:
Left The Reichstag hails Hitler's declaration of war on Poland, 1 September 1939.
Below A Beatles fan hails her beloved.

manifestations to become less political and more private in civilised countries and to be seen only at dances and receptions for film stars or pop singers. The decline of Fascist irrationality, and especially of Hitlerism (the cult of Mussolini created ostentation and buffoonery rather than a truly hysterical mass-exaltation), is shown also in the decline of these huge gatherings, which can now only be collected together, so it seems, by great self-persuasive activity on the part of their organisers.

To resume: communication to large groups through natural channels is becoming less important in Spain; it was

once fundamentally *political*; as the church freed itself progressively from politics and the State, it became merely the place where the devout congregated to worship together; meanwhile *mitines* (meetings) a word which already sounds old-fashioned, though this has nothing I think to do with the fact that the Spanish régime forbids them – have been supplanted by artificial channels of social communication.

16 Artificial channels of mass-communication

The artificial channels of mass-communication are, basically, the press, radio, television, cinema and cheap books. One of the advantages these have over large gatherings has just been suggested: they put an end to pathological crowd-phenomena, collective hysteria and loss of self-control (now hardly to be found except in some youthful gatherings and sporting events, such as football in Spain), when everyone was swept away on a wave of madness under the potent influence of the Führer's screams. Meetings require the audience to make a deliberate decision to attend, to take part in them, whereas television, and even more radio, which does not even have to be looked at, is like an unknown person who intrudes into our house (when perhaps we want to be alone and listen to music) and talks interminably about anything he likes, and just as he likes. It is true that it needs a mere movement of the hand to interrupt him, or that we can be more drastic and refuse to have such an apparatus in our house. But people today, especially the young, feel painfully isolated and alone when deprived of these media of communication and even need them as a background to their studies. At the same time the passion for information grows increasingly more irresistible. These channels are essentially sensory and subject to noise; the newspaper headlines 'scream' just as loudly as the rest, and contribute towards an atmosphere of alienation, as Ortega would call it, typical of town life today.

It has been said that 'freedom consists in being well-informed'. Modern man is eager for information, but it is also necessary to him. Is he in fact well-informed? Contrary to what might be supposed, an excess of undigested informa-

tion, unless it is clarified, analysed and interpreted, can create a superabundance in which the trees of isolated, often contradictory and incoherent pieces of information prevent the wood being seen. We must add to this the fact that every interpretation echoes a 'tendency', and is therefore liable to become 'tendentious'. The only hope of freedom from the first of these limitations lies in the existence of political weeklies, which consider the week's events with a certain detachment, sort out the news items received and re-transmit them according to their importance; and to guard against the second limitation, one needs a free press offering the reader different and opposed interpretations, so that he may make his own choice. But when the press is not under State control, it is usually controlled by huge capitalist enterprises, which tend to interpret the news in very similar ways with slight variations, so that this freedom is more theoretical than real; whereas it is difficult for truly independent periodicals with small circulations to compete, so that their importance and influence is much more 'symbolical' than effective. It is thus only by socialisation of radio and television transmission that freedom to acquire information can be safeguarded today: broadcasts should be 'public services', and all politico–social groups should have equal access to them, whatever their ideology.

According to the now classic questions asked by Lasswell[43] about the media of mass-information, it is necessary to know *who* is saying what is being said, exactly *what* he is really saying, *to whom* it is addressed (i.e. to what 'audience') and what *effects* he is producing.

It is important for instance to know if the *who* can be identified in a totalitarian state with the Ministry of Propaganda or its organs of dissemination, or with agents employed by pressure groups or foreign powers or interests, or particular political parties. An analysis of the content (apart from other private or confidential sources of information) may show whose voice we are really listening to, even though he is trying to conceal himself, or is forced to do so, as happens in totalitarian states where only the voice of officialdom can be heard.

It is easy to discover *to whom* the communication is addressed: there are the workers' newspapers, the middle-class papers, the denominational papers (either official, or acquiescent like *Ya* in Madrid); the party press (Madrid's *Arriba*, the organ of the only legal party); newspapers that are bought for symbolical and establishment reasons rather than for the quality of their news (*ABC* in Madrid); the illustrated magazines, superficial by their very nature, but in which a careful analysis of the content may detect a definite orientation (for example *Actualidad Española*, *Meridiano*); the sensational magazines; sporting and children's magazines; women's magazines (among which we must distinguish important ones like *Elle* and *Marie Claire* from the French *Presse du Coeur* and mere fashion magazines); economic and financial journals (it is interesting to analyse the content of these – for instance Madrid's *España Económica*); 'digests' and 'comics'; cinema magazines (critical or merely commercial); magazines aimed at special audiences, like *Fortune*, *Esquire* and *Playboy* in the United States. It is clear that the more highly evolved a country is, the more diverse and specialised is its press.

We must also bear in mind that the *new* media of communication, especially the most typical cinema and television programmes, are not aimed at the general public. Their 'language' (in the widest sense of the word) is only fully comprehensible to the *new* generation, the young. This is obvious in the case of music, but it also applies to film montage, with its special form of 'syntax', which is too rapid and full of implications for an older audience. Even the language is based on different verbal conventions or implicit judgements of value, and has a different emotional charge, so that parents cannot join their children in looking at some of the cinema and television programmes, or reading 'comics'. Consequently those boys and girls whose parents take special care to keep them away from these media of communication find themselves at a loss in the world of the young and lapse

Mass media: supply keeping up
with demand – and
helping to create it.

into imitative and regressive behaviour.[44] It is probably an exaggeration to describe as the 'subculture' the noticeable effects of the superiority of the young – including mere children – in the *know-how* of manipulating modern gadgets and appreciating and discriminating between the newest types of consumer goods. This all helps to raise a barrier of incomprehension between the generations.

We all know in a general sort of way *what* an organ of dissemination is saying, but when we start analysing its content various problems arise. We must first be quite clear what is to be investigated; next, after assessing the representative sample, we must go on to compute the words used, and the stereotyped associations with them which act as keys; thence to chosen themes, the types of language and vocabulary, the different typographical and stylistic ways of presenting the same piece of news, its readableness or unreadableness, and so forth.[45]

The *effects* of different means of communication are often discussed today. Until a short time ago it was the fashion to denounce the forcible manipulation of opinion, attitudes and behaviour by mass media. Today it is more often held that though mass media undoubtedly influence their audiences, they only do so in the direction the latter already wanted to take; and therefore that the general public exerts an influence and a subsequent re-influence on the controllers of the means of communication. An audience is only easily persuadable when it has not formed an opinion about the subject at issue, or knows little about it. Nor can this audience exactly come under the term 'mass', for it consists of separate groups. Now each individual is much more ‘other-directed’, to use Riesman’s expression, by the ‘in-group’ to which he belongs and which he influences in his turn, than he is passively moved by forceful persuasion. This seems to be indisputable, at least in countries where there is no dictatorship, where numerous permanently open channels of communication and many different intermediate and differential groups exist. The following effects of these media of communication are often seen: periodicals or broadcasts with huge circulations are often obliged to transmit very little real news for fear of displeasing some section of their audience; under a formal or totalitarian régime there may be a levelling out of opinion, leading to ‘apathy’ or private conformism, while the appearances of democracy are preserved; movements of opinion with a ‘bandwagon’ effect may be engineered, or opinions that were once independent influenced in the direction of the accepted view by means of mass-communication; ‘myths’ may be created; there is a move towards frivolity and practical materialism in the general attitude to life; subjects that are both truly important and real are put on one side; currents of opinion opposed to totalitarianism, and the individuals who hold them, are subtly discredited.

Cases of obvious unreliability on the part of artificial media of mass-communication, when orientated in a particular political direction, often produce a compensatory reaction towards natural channels. The voice of the independent churches and its ministers is listened to eagerly and with respect; so are rumours, ‘what everyone is saying’, the latest news, even though no more subject to confirmation than the official bulletins; and citizens who want to know what is really happening in their own country, paradoxically enough fall back on foreign organs of mass-communication, particularly radio broadcasts because of their accessibility.

The extremely ambivalent effects of television are of the greatest interest in view of the present and future importance of this artificial medium of communication.[46] This will be dealt with at the end of the present book.

17 Attempts at direct and personal communication through mass-media

In the last section we spoke of the new 'language' of mass-communication, but we have not sufficiently emphasised one of its characteristics which according to Riesman is typical of the present day: *other-direction*, the hetero-conditioning and hetero-orientation of the individual – of each individual – by the group to which he belongs. To return to the image of social communication as a network of relationships, it seems that modern man is all the time becoming better at receiving and deciphering messages difficult for the old to understand, and then rapidly and efficiently re-transmitting them to other receptors. But though the spirit of criticism towards *other* groups is highly developed, it disappears under the influence of the subtle but irresistible need to be approved and accepted by the individual's peer-group. Herein the conformism or false socialisation of the present day finds its most solid support. The media of mass-communication produce an impersonal 'grouping', from which Riesman thinks only some degree of 'marginality' or new form of 'individualism' can save us.

This explains the reaction towards a 'personal' tone in the more intelligent mass-communication programmes. Even in circulars inviting us to subscribe to such and such a periodical we notice a deliberate attempt to address us *individually*, to have a private conversation if possible with each of us. In the same way some broadcasts assume a 'confidential' tone, as if to create the illusion that the speaker has a personal relation with the listener, and is adjusting his message and directing himself especially to him.

The attempt to communicate directly and personally is

still more apparent in the political sphere. Modern democratic politics are fundamentally representative, and insofar as government is carried out by laws rather than men it is inevitably depersonalised. It is often forgotten that the 'paternal' Spanish dictator, General Primo de Rivera, was one of the first to try and establish direct and personal communication with those he governed. Everything he did was directed by a not very clear awareness – for he was a moderately intuitive but not at all intellectual man – that his government must be founded on an unceremonious 'conversation' with the Spanish people, without intervention from parties, committees, lists of candidates, elections or legislative bodies. His own very Spanish and Andalusian gift for communication led him intuitively and without misgiving to the self-confidence he often expressed in an extreme and unfortunately grotesque form in the *notas oficiosas* he published in the newspapers.

Democracy once used another method of making politics personal, which continued until the Fascist convulsion and may have reached its peak today – or yesterday; this was what Walter Benjamin perspicaciously defined as the 'aestheticisation of politics'.[47] During the nineteenth century, politics consisted of fine rhetorical phrases and romatic gestures produced on the national stage of parliament. Anyone who was not a brilliant speaker could not cut a figure as a politician, nor become a general capable of taking heroic decisions on that other stage, the battlefield; he had no hope of becoming a leader, however intelligent he might be, and was relegated to the role of *éminence grise*.

The birth of a new political technique: F. D. Roosevelt, his setting deliberately casual and homely, drops his voice to microgroup level while giving one of his radio and fireside chats from the White House.

Fascism consisted in using the masses as plastic material – both in the sense that they could be moulded at will by the Duce's or Führer's aesthetic or histrionic powers of fascination, and that they were susceptible to the plastic value of aesthetic and rhythmic manifestations.

However the relation between Caudillo and people could never be, or appear to be, an authentically personal one. The crowd was carried away, dominated, fascinated and passively led according to the fancy of the producer of the great public spectacle. The men filing in front of him were merely 'raw material' like the canons, but human raw material. Probably Roosevelt was the first man who understood how to give a personal tone to mass-communication – the radio, in his case – by talking from his own home, from the fireside of the White House, to millions of American homes, in simple direct and personal terms. Later on, Kennedy, making the most of his personal glamour, and De Gaulle, relying on

Television has replaced the political mass-meeting – but has led to conformism and 'other direction' of the individual.

his prestige and rhetoric about the greatness of France, tried various means of profiting by the illusion of direct contact given by television. De Gaulle also made use of that fictitious procedure of direct democracy – a national referendum.

18 The network of channels of communication

The sociology of communication (in its widest sense as the establishment of relations) is concerned with every kind of 'network of communications'. An immeasurably better network is obviously available to us today than in former times, what with motorways, railways, shipping and airlines; daily papers, magazines, large cheap editions of the best – and worst – books; telephone and telegraph, radio, radar and television. And in the probably not far distant future we shall see inter-planetary communication as well. People who were only a short while ago isolated in inaccessible villages, can now keep themselves promptly informed about what is happening in the world, by listening to the radio and looking at television. As has often been said, an age of truly universal history is now beginning, when an event happening in the remotest region can be at once communicated and have repercussions upon the fate of the whole world. Such solidarity between men all over the world has never before been dreamt of. We are all engaged on the same adventure, and the invention and spread of atomic weapons has come to sharpen our awareness of the fact.

But there are various groups still in existence – great blocs, nations, races, and social classes. Multiplicity and non-conformity are opposed to the Russo–American ideals of 'conformity', 'adjustment' and 'consensus of opinion', and create a very necessary element of social dynamism; in this sense Riesman's advocacy of 'individualism', and his defence of privacy and 'marginality' are fully justified. Truly progressive, living democracy is the result of a dialectic between socialisation (or communication in the widest sense) and individualism, 'marginality' and nonconformity.

Democracy (if extended beyond the purely political concept) is a struggle to keep open the network of channels of information and allow communication to flow through them with complete freedom in both directions, in spite of the opposing forces of privilege, monopoly and secrecy. We have already seen that information and entropy exist in inverse ratio to one another. According to Norbert Wiener[48] and what might be called his cosmological metaphysics, the entire world is subject to the second law of thermodynamics and communication is no exception; and when noise, interference and confusion irretrievably destroy a piece of information, it suffers a 'decline' like every other form of energy, towards a static equilibrium or entropy (here the thermodynamic acceptance of this word connects with that of the theory of information) – in fact to death. Hence, according to Wiener, the optimistic belief in Progress as a sort of limitless evolution – a belief that is only two centuries old – is in reality extremely naive. The universe is at least essentially dramatic. But in the midst of this general loss and consumption of energy there are temporal and spatial 'islands' of decreasing entropy, organic in origin and for the most part human – islands where natural energy is liberated, where homoeostasis or dynamic equilibrium is produced, and individual and cosmic life exists. In the struggle for life – not in the Darwinian sense as we shall see – the attempt to liberate energy and information in the teeth of the continual threat of entropy, the desire for activity and communication, constitute the noblest destiny of man in this world. He is utterly involved, he is wedded to liberty and also to a sort of philosophical faith: that expressed in Einstein's words, 'Der Herr Gott ist raffiniert aber boshaft ist Er nicht'. Whoever presides over our destinies – God, Nature, Physis or whatever name is chosen – is subtle, and incomprehensible, and enjoys the conflict between the upwards and downwards forces, but is not, for all that, evil. And, unlike all other tyrants (including those who pretend to be patriarchal or protective) he leaves us completely free during our lives. That is why the human adventure is greater than any other.

Part 3

The sociology of communication: the content

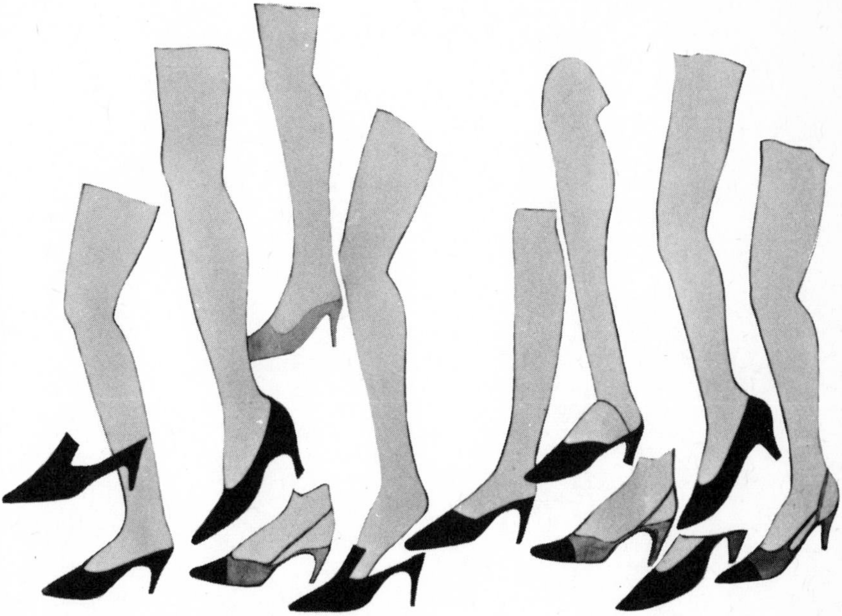

19 Language and non-communication

In the previous chapter we saw how the channels used alter the very character of the social communication. In the present chapter we shall be studying not *how* communication is established but *what* is communicated, the nature of the content of the communication and the sociological importance of different types of communication.

It will not be out of place to begin by a rapid survey of language itself, just as we did in the previous chapter, not now as a channel of communication *par excellence*, but with reference to its content; we shall then go on to study the different types of informative content. But first we must consider the question of the veracity or otherwise of language, and whether its intention is to give accurate information or distort the content of the communication. For language can be used to disguise messages as well as to transmit them. It disguises them, of course, by encoding them, in case those for whom they were not intended should intercept them; but also in order to conceal them from the addressees themselves, and even from the emitters.

There are evidently messages that are not intended to be understood, or rather that have no real content. A politician who is anxious to get out of a tight corner and fills his speeches with commonplaces and vague expressions that amount to nothing; a diplomat who talks merely to gain time until he receives exact instructions; a pseudo-thinker who conceals reality beneath 'ideas' that are totally alien to it – these are a few examples of the many instances of such use of language.

Things may be carried even further: in a given social

situation language may conceal reality from the emitter himself as well as the receptor. Bacon's 'idols' and the ideologies of modern sociological philosophy, are instances of this; and on a personal level a constitutional tendency to conceal the truth from oneself, the existential hypocrisy that Sartre called 'mauvaise foi', fulfils the same function. No one can in fact thoroughly deceive other people unless he has first deceived himself, or at least come to believe his own lie in the course of the process. Machiavellism rationalises an operation which would be weakened by analysis and self-criticism. A flagrant lie casts a shadow around itself and secretes its own anaesthetic, or at least its own self-justification – fanaticism is an example of this. Men contrive to live reasonably well in this tenebrous world where truth and falsehood are confounded in one blurred vision. Language is not only the chief means of communication; it is also the most effective way to falsify real communication thereby leading to non-communication.

Language may also be non-communicative to large numbers of possible receptors because of the special idiom or jargon it makes use of, or the very nature of what is communicated. In fact no universal language comprehensible by everyone exists. Each language communicates to those who speak it, at the cost of leaving the rest uninformed. There exist today special jargons belonging to every occupation, and serving as communication among those who practise it though difficult for outsiders to understand. And finally there are linguistic contents which cannot be understood without apprenticeship, not so much on account of the words but of the reality, the experience they refer to. Scientific and aesthetic communication provide two completely different forms of this 'apprenticeship'.

There are other more complicated problems concerning communication however. Every message (or use of language) has its place, as has been shown, in the whole behaviour-series, and in a context of previous assumptions. A knowledge of these presuppositions is the only thing that can lead to understanding of the message or language. But knowledge is always interpretation, and this in turn involves an element of volition; the knowledge-interpretation has to be accepted.

On the other hand, because of the pressure of society on the individual, his mental processes are profoundly conditioned by the habits of thought and view of reality of his in-group, or the group to which he belongs, which functions also as a reference-group in relation to those outside it, or the out-group.

Two examples taken from the present political situation in Spain may be used to illustrate this. One is the dilemma, ever explicitly or implicitly present, between Communism and the present régime. This dilemma, surprisingly enough, excludes a third which is extremely widespread in the Western world: democracy. How can this be understood by anyone who has not made the hermeneutic assumption that the history of modern Spain 'demonstrates' that a democracy is impossible in that country, that it always leads to anarchy, and that the only possible solution is either Communism or dictatorship; and that the Second Republic and the Civil War provided the *experimentum crucis* which 'verified' the inescapableness of this dilemma?

Our second example refers to the slogan so constantly produced in Spain in 1964 about 'twenty-five years of Peace'. It might be thought more realistic to speak of 'twenty-five years of Victory', for how can one speak of peace – which must be, above all, spiritual peace – when we are living on constantly evoked memories of the war and on constant discrimination between 'good' and 'bad' Spaniards according to the side they were on, which was often a matter of pure chance?

It is evidently the in-group which deliberately imposes this version of reality, according to which, even if democracy is not considered as bad or false, as it often is, it is held to be impossible here and now. With this goes the belief that Peace is synonymous with material Order resulting from Victory, and that all possible opposition or deviation, however moderate, must be excluded.

Now if we all belong to some in-group or other, which can be taken as our identification-mark, how can we ever escape from it and from the interpretations of reality it imposes on us? It is the special function of intellectuals to criticise all apparently obvious and unquestioned assumptions – I am not of course referring only to politics. An intellectual is someone who is capable either of emerging from the social group to which he belongs, or else of criticising it from within. His most difficult task is to submit the fundamental 'beliefs' of his own group to implacable analysis. How can he do this? Only by not being fully integrated with his group and by being therefore only partly subjected to its social pressure. (Many pseudo-intellectuals are completely subjugated by their social group, however.) In the case of those who belong to several in-groups simultaneously, the various 'cross-pressures', as American sociologists call them, compensate for one another and produce a certain degree of liberty. This happens for instance to Catholics who belong to the Socialist party, Englishmen who are not Anglicans, and Americans who are not 'WASPS'.[49] Pluralism is the instrument of liberation, because it neutralises what would otherwise be unilateral or totalitarian social pressure.

A classification of the content of information must distinguish between communication that is scientific and technological, informative, propagandist, educational, aesthetic, social-economical, political, international and oecumenical.

20 Scientific and technological communication

Until very recent times, and in particular until the rise of technology, the most remarkable characteristic of science has been its attitude of apparently complete 'disinterestedness'. Science was *theoria* or contemplation to the Greeks, and 'knowledge' to Galileo and Newton. But even to the latter the Greek inheritance of *epistemê* and *technê* were quite distinct from one another. In other ancient civilisations, Egyptian or Babylonian for instance, things were probably different, and their 'science' arose from practical needs. Just because it was at once made the slave of its practical application, it failed to develop as it did in the West. The typically Hellenic notion of 'knowledge for knowledge's sake', of *epistemê* as a function of pure *theoria*, was necessary as a rational device by which science was to be set free from slavery to immediate needs, and develop as a sort of intellectual 'game'. Technical skills, on their part, developed quite independently, either by chance or under pressure from everyday experience, and from the ingenuity and industry of those who had to deal with practical necessities such as the division of labour, its economy and progress.

The transition from the eighteenth to the nineteenth century was the great period of invention in technique and craftsmanship. Technical skills progressed by means of 'accidents' or 'expedients' based on general scientific principles to whose discovery and formulation they had not contributed. The real advances of the nineteenth century came with the beginning of *technology*, when science was deliberately applied to the domination of nature, and applied science resulted. Auguste Comte was the prophet of the new technological age; he realised that the purpose of science was not to contemplate the universe and its laws with detachment, but to discover how to apply the laws of nature so as to influence the world, foresee events and provide for the future. Thus *science* became *power*. In this respect Comte's philosophy of science had an absolutely decisive effect. However the nineteenth century did not organise itself according to Auguste Comte's theories, which though far from liberal were in agreement with the economic principle of Free Trade. The idea of 'absolute property' was transferred from the land to industry by means of the notions of 'work' and 'value', and naturally involved scientific inventions with immediately obvious practical applications. Thus originated the concept of 'intellectual property' in the form of inventions, registered under a patent, put on the market and finally acquired by large industrial firms. The process of evolution from free science and improvements in technique and craftsmanship to this traffic or trade in scientific invention has been studied by the philosopher P. Dominique Dubarle. But such a development does not end there, as he and others have realised. Great industries have at last understood that the purchase of inventions is a bad system: 'exploitation of science' must follow the example of 'exploitation of industry', but the fabulous resources needed were far beyond the reach of the scientist who used to work on his own in a rudimentary laboratory set up at his own expense in some room unsuitable as a classroom. The romantic and heroic period of the great independent scientists, such as Ramon y Cajal in Spain, is already over. Two possibilities remain: the astonishing developments in the United States, where, still on the lines of a Liberal economy, the great industries form research departments and employ scientists to work at high salaries and with splendid equipment, so creating research institutes backed by private enterprise and definitely industrial in aim like the Bell Telephone Company, General Electric, Westinghouse, Rand Corporation, IBM, etc. A second possibility is that *liberty* is given primacy over *property*, and huge technological institutes affiliated to private universities are created, such as MIT. This last method perpetuates the Liberal scheme, without converting science and its findings into an 'industrial property'.

The next step was the nationalisation of research. The École Pratique des Hautes Études and the Centre National de la Recherche Scientifique in France, and their Spanish simulacrum (in nearly all departments) the Consejo Superior de Investigaciones Cientificas, are carrying out a severance between the State University as a teaching centre and the State institutes of research, while still respecting their relationship – a felicitous formula, in my opinion, for combining 'nationalisation' and 'liberty'. But liberty is easily sacrificed, especially in the field of atomic research, where in order that warlike aims should prevail over pacific ones, science is in process of becoming militarised and regimented. And not only in this field: aims that may not be military but are undoubtedly political are adopted by certain national institutes (of statistics, demography and – in Spain, where it cannot be expressed – of public opinion) and placed at the source of non-scientific interests; and once they have been taken over by politics they are withdrawn from open communication such as was dealt with at the end of the last chapter. The 'patented' secrets of the old days have today been replaced by 'military' ones, or by political 'propaganda'. Where once we had industrial ambitions, we now have the State trying to obstruct scientific channels of communication. Experience has shown that both these ambitions are doomed to failure; rivals and enemies alike always discover our secrets in the end, and usually without having recourse to espionage. It is on the scientific 'level' that so-called technological secrets are mainly disseminated today. Norbert Wiener has emphasised the fact that science is a game (not in the playful sense alluded to previously, but as a struggle against an adversary).[50] The free scientist, matching himself against Nature, can rest assured that he has an 'adversary' who cannot discover his methods and strategy and so alter the line of attack; whereas the regimented scientist has to follow regular strategic lines as in the theory of games, in order to hide his own discoveries and reach his proposed objective before the scientists of other nations.

This situation sets the modern scientist several serious moral problems. The first is the loss of his autonomy. He can no longer follow his own bent. Modern research needs such a vast financial outlay that he has to join some research institute, which, as we have seen, may belong to an industry or be under State or military control. The first and third of these situations by their very nature deprive him of the power to communicate with other scientists, lest he betray the business or country he is working for. And he realises that research and information are subject to the *decisions* of others. He has become simply an 'expert', working for a salary, he does not exactly know to what end, but possibly – in the third case – for the extermination of the entire human race against his will. This 'exploitation' of science and scientists has been clearly pointed out by Chombart de Lauwe with regard to the human sciences: 'If we are not careful, the sciences of decision may set themselves up against the sciences of information . . . instead of complementing them'.[51] By fighting for communication between men of science of all nations we can make one of the most effective contributions to the cause of world peace.

The sociology of communication is also concerned with problems of another type, less dramatic than these but no less difficult. One of them is that of the accurate reception and assimilation of scientific information. The scientist of today is overwhelmed by information, but lack of time, memory or psycho-physiological energy prevent him making use of it. The output of scientific literature at the present day is immense. Obviously science must be subdivided, a specialised field given to each scientist and his team of research-workers. However there are gaps between the different branches of scientific research, through which may slip scientific messages that are of particular interest, because they open new avenues of thought to those who usually move in too restricted ambits of knowledge.[52] It is true that an attempt is being made to bridge these gaps by studying the relations between special fields. It is also true that much scientific research is redundant. The academic 'curriculum', and the necessity of publishing something, force many scientists who have not yet gained a reputation to emit communications that are quite unnecessary. In any case the problem is a genuine one, and can only be solved by means of the socialisation of scientific research and a wider and more effective use of electronic apparatus capable of registering and recording information that the human brain cannot contain.

The subject of electronic apparatus leads us to another sociological problem – the relationship of the modern scientist to his instruments, and the social and human repercussions of this relationship. In the seventeenth century people believed that God, the Great Watchmaker, had wound up the world at the beginning of time, and they wanted to get as close as possible to the ideal of *perpetuum mobile*. Now it is a question of following this 'antique' model by creating instruments that can be strictly controlled or tele-controlled by man and so extend his powers of action. Cybernetics, automation, and the theory of information have profoundly modified the old relation between man and machine. Where once he managed and tended an automatic apparatus and adapted himself to its rhythm, he is now the creator of self-directing machines that have been given partial autonomy. The problem, from our point of view, is how man is to communicate with these new machines. He must carry out a planned 'programme', which for our purposes consists in 'talking' to the computer or electronic calculating-machine in a 'language' it can 'understand'. Until a short while ago this had to be 'written' on perforated cards

Below Information and control: A punched card, part of the computer's 'program' or language medium.
Right Man in control of the information supplied to him.

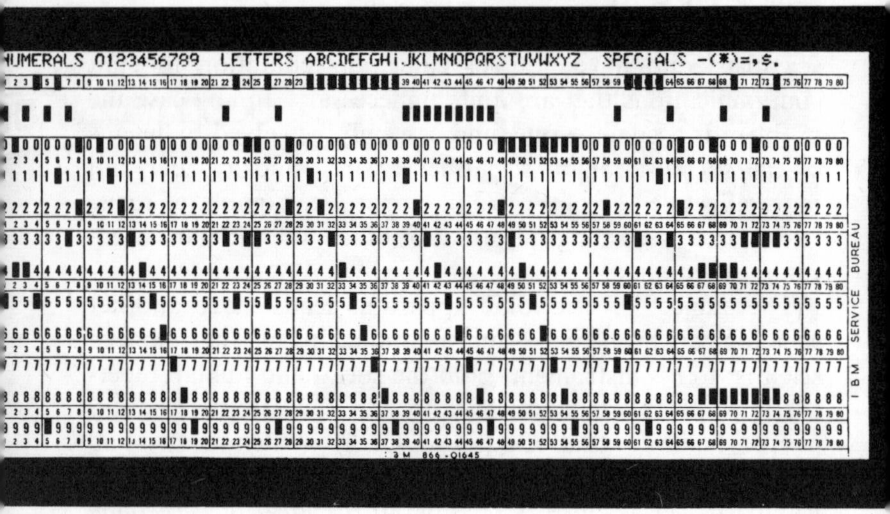

or numerals (digital computers). In this way the 'conversation' between the scientist and his electronic apparatus is much like that between professor and student during an examination: in both cases the *answers* are based on a programme. But there is an important difference: the machine makes some replies that were previously totally unknown to the professor. As we shall see in Part Four, by generalising this relationship and giving it an ordinary, everyday significance, the very developed countries are tending to destroy its mythical character. The super-human 'electronic brain', so hair-raising in science fiction, is today becoming diminished, more submissive and accommodating and within the reach of everyone – largely through British efforts in this

direction. By means of portable 'terminals' (such as 'teletypewriters' for recording questions) which are connected with the 'time-sharing systems' of powerful computers installed in great research institutes, every humble user can partake of the knowledge in these central stores – whether by telephone, radio or television – while at the same time augmenting those stores by his collaboration. Thus, as we shall see at the end of this book, we are abandoning the fantastic vision of wretched human beings driven by gigantic thinking and judging machines wherever their automatic whims direct. As always, it is not domination by machines we need fear, but by men – dictators.

We have already indirectly referred to the problem of how

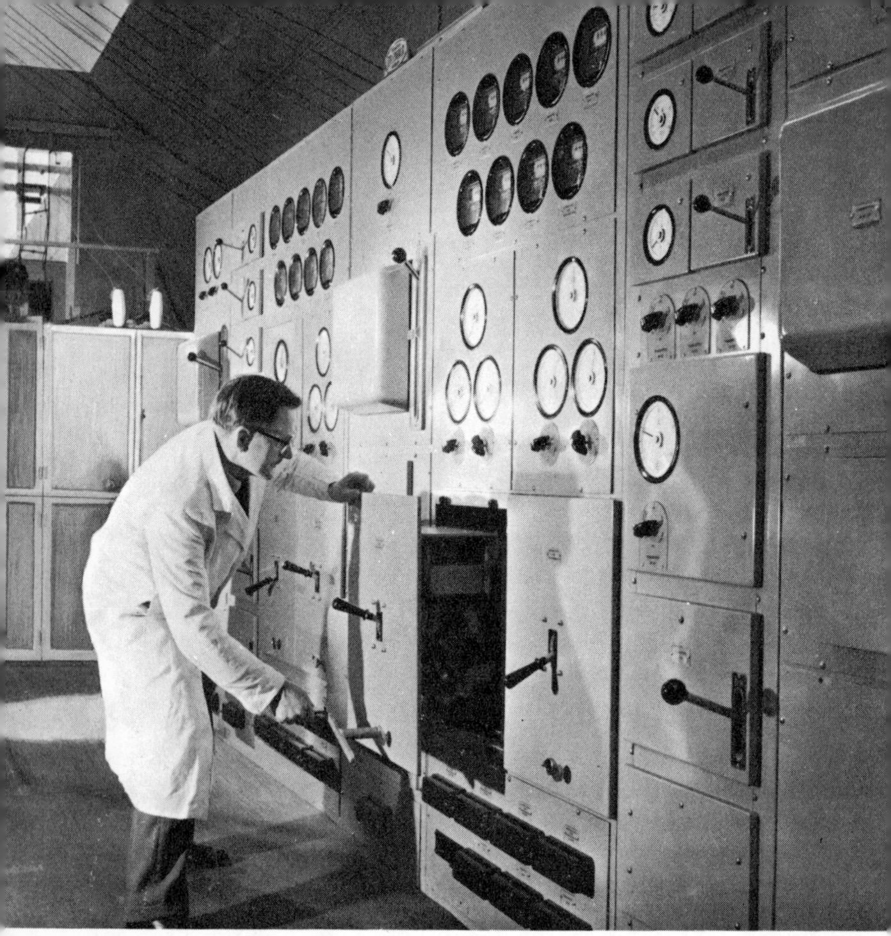

research – which as we saw should be free – can be harnessed to social needs, to the 'carrying out of orders' (more profitable than pure science) or the claims of 'development'. Here we have a more subtle form of pressure than the direct regimentation of scientists mentioned just now, but both tend to the same result – the primacy of the applied over the pure sciences.

In theory one way of avoiding these difficulties is obviously for the great research institutes to be subsidised by the State but not under its control, and to function as public services, affiliated in some way to the universities while retaining their independence and separate purpose. But strongly held opinions are brought forward to oppose the liberty of science – social, moral and patriotic considerations, and even the defence of civilisation (whether Christian, Western or Socialist); the struggle is hard and will probably become even more so.

21 Communication of news and publicity

International networks of communication have in these last years become infinitely more dense than before, and the various regions of the world are now so closely interconnected that, in spite of the differences between nations or blocs of nations, news which can for the first time in history be described as 'planetary' – news about the maintenance of an unstable world equilibrium or threats to it, about the frictions each day produces, the fresh hopes, and events that seem harmless at first sight but full of significance on analysis – can be immediately transmitted in every direction throughout this complicated network of communications.

But who gives us our information? The press, radio, television. Now, as everyone knows, these mass media of communication cannot, any more than a business, be profitable without publicity. Information is supplied free to the public by radio and television, and much below cost by the press. So that mass media of communication have to be kept alive by publicity and are to an increasing degree controlled by advertisers. It is also relevant to remember what was said in Part One about the reciprocal influence between the supposed 'manipulators' and the 'manipulated'. News and communications for publicity purposes are thus seen to be intimately linked, to such an extent that it is very often impossible to tell whether a press report about a film-star, a bathing-beach which is just becoming the rage, or a new industrial plant ('the pride of our country and eloquent proof of that progress which has set us on an equality with the most advanced nations') is a news item disinterestedly offered to the reader, or publicity to keep the periodical or broadcasting station alive. There recently appeared in English, within the space of a few months, one whole number of a review (*Holiday*) and two supplements to daily papers (*The Guardian* and *The New York Times*) entirely dedicated to Spain. The first was a survey or interpretation of the country which had nothing to do with publicity. Nor did the second originally, but in the end it was flooded with so much publicity from official sources that some of the articles commissioned and paid for had to be omitted. The third was unadulterated propaganda backed by the Spanish government. But the word 'advertisement' was printed in such tiny type that it was hardly visible. Other periodicals do without this announcement altogether, and only mark the difference between information and publicity by means of conventional signs or phrases such as 'communicated by a correspondent', which can only be interpreted by careful readers who are also in the know.

There is another reason why the frontier between information and propaganda is hard to fix: political interference. Every event is significant, but its significance is rarely unequivocal: it requires to be interpreted with a complete objectivity which is aimed at but hardly ever attained. Each periodical interprets events according to its own standpoint, or, in countries where the press is not free, according to the dictates of the government. The distinction between organs of information and organs of opinion is purely relative. Organs of information are no less conditioned by interest than those of opinion; it is merely that the interests are of a different sort – economic rather than political. Aimed at a vast audience having nothing in common except that they all belong to the 'general public', they have to avoid subjects which might lose them a great many readers, keep their information within a neutral zone where controversial messages are reduced to an indispensable minimum, and provide instead a diet of entertainment and evasiveness.

A further, linguistic proof of the extreme difficulty, not to say impossibility, of distinguishing between 'information' and 'publicity' or 'propaganda' is seen in the overlap between the meanings of the three words. The dictionary definition of 'publicity' is the quality or state of being public, and the means of making a thing public through information or communication. Etymologically, 'propaganda' is the action of propagating – that is to say diffusion or information. However, except in very special contexts, such as 'give publicity to' (synonymous with 'make public') or the Latin 'propaganda Fidei', 'propaganda' or 'publicity' is understood to mean an announcement in the press or for transmission by telecommunication advertising a product or service and paid for by the dealer or manufacturer, not as diffusion of news or information. But, by a compensatory inversion of meanings, political propaganda – which deserves the name just as much as the commercial sort – has shaken off its name, and what used to be the Ministry of Propaganda is today the Ministry of Information.

Studies known as 'motivational research' have also revealed psychological devices used by those dispensing information, exactly like those used by radio announcers. Both try to take us out of our small, humdrum everyday world and convey us into another that is more exciting, dream-like or sensational. A good advertiser promises us a 'new life', richer and more intense than our usual one, if we spend our summer holiday on this beach or that cruise. But a good foreign correspondent transports us in imagination to the far-off country where he is, perhaps the same one to which the air and shipping lines want to carry us. One has only to remember what was said in Part One about 'contemporary mythologies', and to re-read the Works of Roland Barthes and Edgar Morin, and this point will be immediately understood. Can anyone who does not possess the right 'keys' distinguish the advertisement pages from the rest in one of the large illustrated magazines devoted to conveying the pleasant side of life? Every page in the whole production carries out an identical function.

The thirst for trifling, but not uninteresting information corresponds to the same psychological need as publicity. It is clear that most of the information transmitted by mass media of communication is worthless. Yet it performs a psychological function, for good or ill, which cannot be gone into here. Human curiosity has always been attracted by the idea of 'being a witness', 'being on the spot', 'seeing a thing with one's own eyes'. To watch something actually happening – this is the fascination exerted by 'direct' transmission, as Marcello Rodino has rightly stressed.[53] Mass media of communication with a conservative orientation may be used to distract a politically opposed audience with 'details' and 'anecdotes', and so provide 'actuality', instead of that 'distance' which makes it easier to see things as a whole and take in their meaning. The special view of life thus provided is however put across in all 'good faith', since those responsible, far from being averse to spreading 'fragmentary' or 'insignificant' information throughout the world, feel it to be necessary.

Modern man *seeks* information just as he seeks publicity. To denounce the latter as deliberate 'manipulation' is almost as ingenuous as the declaration by the eighteenth-century Encyclopedists that religion must have been invented by physically weak but very astute men (the priests) for it to be able to manipulate people. Whether one believes in it or not, religion corresponds to a collective mental structure. In just the same way, publicity is a fundamental part of an economic structure – the 'economy of consumption', which must be ceaselessly increased, so that the wheels of production shall not stop revolving. Now this is not a purely economic pattern of life but also a social and in its way moral one, which is spreading further and further throughout the world, at least through what is called the Western world, and even sometimes setting up infection in the opposing bloc. The desire to be well-informed and 'up to date' (often about very unimportant things) is not very different from the desire to stand out from the crowd by smoking cigarettes or wearing shirts which, according to the advertisers, mark one as being 'up to date' as a consumer of the latest novelties (also a matter of very slight importance). The public *finds* in information and publicity exactly what it is *looking for*, though often without realising the fact. This is the reason behind the growth of a species of applied research known as market forecasting. Of course to suppose that publicity has no effect at all on the public would be to fall into the opposite error. But this influence always moves in the same *direction* towards which the public is feeling its way. And the influence is reciprocal.[54] What is happening in the case of publicity really applies to everything else. As was said from the first and will be seen in more detail at the end of this book, the historical outlook of today is not retrospective but prospective, projected into the future. Prospecting – whether for oil or trade – is merely the micro-economic dimension of the completest possible forecasting and planning of the future.

To contradict the old saying that 'good wine needs no bush', and regard consumers' greed as an invention of advertising agencies, is like supposing that the 'hurry' of modern life was invented by motor-car and aeroplane manufacturers. Modern man needs to consume time, money and information, without pause. This is all part of the intimate structure of a 'way of life' which may or may not be to our taste, but is the one Western man has adopted.

If the moral issue still seems relevant, I will apply it in concrete terms, *hic et nunc*, to present-day Spain. Spain is now at the cross-roads, on the point of entering fully into the way of life described above, with the remotely possible alternative of adopting the Marxist version, and a third of realising a 'revolution towards freedom' or 'democratic socialism', thus taking a middle course of its own, as we have suggested, which would be both modern and moral. The countries of the two great blocs have already chosen their respective courses. We still have time to choose one that is truly ours – an extremely difficult task, but not impossible.

22 Pedagogic communication

Education is the most fundamental means of socialisation and therefore of communication. The other forms of communication we have examined may be more evolved *technologically* than communication through teaching, but where *content* is concerned pedagogic communication is the chief factor contributing to a country's integration, stability and progress, and its socio-economic and political structures are functions of it. It is the underdeveloped countries, in which modern scientific and technological education is lacking, that have no political stability and succumb to autocratic forms of government, as S. M. Lipset has shown; and the same result is arrived at where there is no underdevelopment but where economic misfortune has been overlaid with an extravagant 'mythology' resulting in real cultural regression, such as happened in Hitler's Germany. The relation between social stratification and education will be dealt with later; and pedagogic communication is of course dependent on information and scientific research.[55]

Education plays a decisive part in communication – or non-communication: a) by establishing the values of society as a whole and of its different sub-groups; b) by integration and compartmentalisation; and c) within the same scholastic community. Education in fact consists in transmitting standards of behaviour, both scientific-technical (instruction) and moral (character-formation), that can either be shared by all members of a society or differentiated according to some criterion of stratification; either within a single school or with free choice of education; and with greater or less cohesion between students and teachers – that is to say a variable degree of identification with the school.

But it would be quite wrong to assume that the only medium of education is the one civilised countries have formally adopted – school, beginning with the primary grade and ending with the higher grades, and the universities. In primitive societies no such formal or 'academic' course exists; while in modern communities we find, alongside it, informal media of education based on family, church, society and social life: the acquisition of ordinary and professional skills; what is learnt from the organisation of labour (the techniques learnt at work, the feelings of solidarity originating in factories and expressed in trades unions) and from bureaucracy and the order necessarily imposed by modern life and town life in particular (municipal administration, traffic control, census, registration, records, manifestos, petitions, etc., etc.). And today we must add to family, church and society, mass media of communication.

The family is the primary entity of communication; it transmits the sub-culture and religion of the social group it belongs to, and within it a profound process of socialisation takes place. There is parental communication and adaptation to the parents' life; the children are brought up in the bosom of the family, where the parents' religious, moral, cultural and patriotic values are embodied, the most elementary techniques of bodily hygiene are acquired, and family feeling is aroused. But a family is not always fully integrated, and even when it is, this integration nowadays less often takes a monolithic form. Where there is a 'mixed marriage' each of the parents has a different religion, and very often at least

one of the two has none; there may be more or less serious quarrelling between them; and as for the children, each has a completely different attachment to the family cell according to his chronological position among the rest – whether first-born, younger brother, the Benjamin (who may also be 'the unwanted one'), or according to sex – the only girl among boys, or the only male child among a lot of sisters – or character and behaviour. There may be tension between the generations as well as between siblings. The children have to live in two separate worlds – the adult world represented by their parents and their friends, and that of other children;[56] they do not *yet* think or feel like adults, least of all like their parents. The family is thus the first school of communication, but also of tension, toleration, discussion, adaptation and disagreement; and it too often also provides – in the form of divorce, desertion and serious quarrels – the first experience of non-communication, disintegration and broken relationships.

In periods and countries where religious unity prevailed, the church was a powerful factor in communication, integration and communion. Today the diversity of faiths, de-Christianisation, and the general agnosticism if not atheism, are taking us further and further away from this solidarity of the old days, and giving society a pluralist form. It is the same with modern man's religion as with family life or his relation to society: he seems destined to form a community oscillating between satisfactory communication and the threat of disintegration – in other words to live in a dynamic and changing social equilibrium.

Surgery is one of many subjects to benefit from teaching methods using closed-circuit television and other electronic means.

Through mass media of communication education has today become notoriously important, and many modern sociologists speak of 'mass culture' as if it were opposed to, or different from, scholastic culture. In backward countries innumerable people who have hardly set foot in an elementary school get all their information from radio, television, periodicals and paperbacks, which make the works of great thinkers and writers available to all. These are an important medium of informal pedagogic communication.[57]

Besides their informal value, books have ever since their invention been very important as *formal* means of communication, and other mass media are just beginning to follow suit. Regular courses of purely instructive programmes given on radio and television, and the electronic information now available for educational purposes, have opened new perspectives of formal teaching, and will in the near future radically transform it, above all in relation to new scholastic methods, adult education in a changing society[58] and 'continuous education'. This will be dealt with in our last chapter; it has become a real need of the present day.

We must next consider formal education proper – namely schools.

The chief characteristics of school teaching are its grading of progress – in which it differs from the disorganised instruction provided by mass media of communication; and its 'rationality' (the fact that it requires pupils to 'use their reason') – in which it differs from *training* or mere acquisition of skills, indoctrination for service under some political organisation, and the more or less spontaneous incorporation

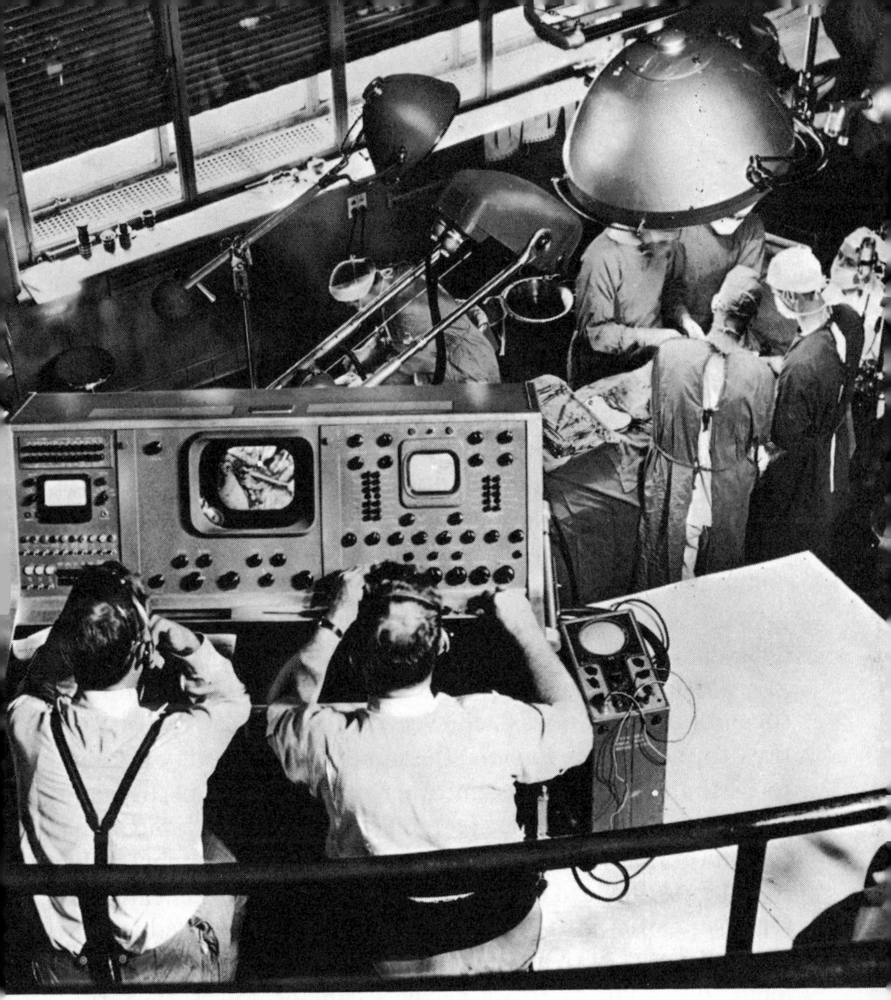

of the culture of another race, either because it is considered superior, or by simple 'contagion' based on a superiority that is felt rather than clearly perceived.

We find in modern schools, as in the family and other informal educational structures, that tension between integration and disintegration, that dynamics of constant change so characteristic of the ever accelerating history of our times. Communication and non-communication co-exist, as we have said, in social classes, society as a whole, and inside the schools themselves and the scholastic community. Let us examine each of these in turn.

It seems clear that the division of teaching into three grades – primary, secondary and higher – corresponds to the desire of the bourgeoisie to maintain a certain cultural non-communication[59] or monopoly, as well as to its trichotomous view of society (lower, middle and upper class) – the intermediate 'middle class' to act as a shock-absorber between the *two* classes of Marxism.[60] The bourgeois form of political-social organisation was achieved through education. In contrast to the *Ancien Régime*, the upper class of today appears to be the educated class, in other words the propertied and managerial bourgeoisie (capitalists). But do riches and education *really* coincide? They must do so if the new order is to be justified. (There is a social implication beneath this scholastic situation: only through enlightenment, education and culture – not of a humanistic sort or as mere accomplishment, but adapted to its needs – can the lower class rise, individually and collectively. And in the same way, as everyone now realises, it is only by education, enlightenment and culture – not literary or 'metaphysical' but technological – that economic progress can continue.) If therefore they do not coincide of their own accord, they must be made to at all costs. Primary education was therefore mainly designed for the lower classes, secondary education for the middle classes, and higher education reserved exclusively for the upper classes. (Liberalism knew how to deceive itself whenever the necessary correlations were not spontaneously produced.) Thus ownership of property – and its sequel, full citizenship for ratepayers – was made to coincide with full education and social-political class-superiority 'justified' by superior education and wealth. In *La barrière et le niveau*, Goblot clearly saw that bourgeois schools performed the double function of raising a 'barrier' that could not be crossed by the lower classes, and establishing various levels that were concerned at the same time with social status and intellectual attainment. The educational system fulfilled the double function of stratified integration – in which property and education (or lack of them) and social class were closely connected – and of thoroughly 'sifting' or 'filtering', so that only exceptionally gifted individuals were able to raise themselves to a higher educational level and thus free themselves from their original class and join a higher one. In this way the educational system went on being stratified at three levels – a reasonably good solution, since it maintained the tension between the classes while preventing it becoming too violent thanks to the 'mediation' of the middle class and the possibility of intellectual self-advancement, and a moral one in that to belong to the upper class did not appear as a privilege (as with the *Ancien Régime*) but as the 'result' of superior education. Pierre Bourdieu and Jean-Claude Passeron[61] have recently shown that, quite apart from the economic 'barrier', the structure and even the content of studies, and (as we shall see later) the very 'language' in which the educational

message is communicated (close to that of the upper class and completely different from that of the lower) gives an advantage that may not be obvious, but is hard to overcome to students from middle-class homes in preference to those of proletarian or lower-middle class extraction.

Today things are tending to change: first, perhaps, because no other country has seen such an 'intellectualisation' of the middle classes as is typical of France, and above all because

Bourgeois schools and colleges, with their shared associations and special 'language', have been an important factor historically in segregating the upper classes of society from the lower. *Left* Eton boys. *Below* Heidelberg students (*circa* 1900) in duelling outfit.

present-day culture, being increasingly scientific and technological in orientation, cancels out the initial advantage enjoyed by upper-class students and even turns it to the disadvantage of the 'leisured classes'. So that, if the economic barrier is withdrawn, there will for the first time exist all the conditions needed to make education a genuine channel of communication between the classes and productive of social mobility.

Besides a tendency to increased social communication between classes in civilised Western countries, we find an increase of the *actual time* given to compulsory education, and also that a larger number of young people from the lower classes can now go to universities. No one now declares, openly at least, that one has to belong to the upper class to get into university or one of the better schools, although *in fact* it is still sometimes true. The *theoretical* problems of today takes a different form. If education is taken to be a long-term *investment* for progress,[62] is it more profitable to concentrate the economic resources devoted to it on the most gifted, whatever class they come from, and make of them by means of what Pareto calls 'the circulation of the élite' an 'upper class' chosen on strictly intellectual and technological grounds, or to keep closer to the democratic ethos, though probably less profitably, by making as much education as possible available to all, and so raising the cultural level of the whole country? We are here faced with a question of principle, to be decided according to which is valued most highly, technological-economic productivity or real and effective democracy – in other words, whether economics or morals are given primacy. Of course in practice compromise solutions are generally adopted: it is formally announced that education must become fully democratic, but when the time comes a series of artificial and 'intellectual' obstacles arise, and so much time and money is expended in surmounting them that they indirectly help to preserve the system of privilege in favour of boys from the economically and socially more powerful classes referred to above.

Schools are social institutions and therefore part of society as a whole. But what relation exists between the schools (or the educational subsystem), the social system and the pedagogic Establishment, or official educational subsystem? We said before that education was the transmission of behaviour-patterns. These are based on cultural or moral values, recognised as such by society. But modern society differs from primitive and traditional societies in being not unitary but pluralist. The pedagogic Establishment or official educational subsystem rests upon certain established values and imposes the behaviour-patterns founded on them. These values and patterns may not now correspond to the *real* structure of society and its needs and aspirations. If in spite of this the schools continue to adhere to them, the current of living culture will flow through new and more suitable channels. This is what happened to European universities at the time of the Renaissance. Realising that they were stagnating in scholasticism, the culture of the period turned away from them, and was transferred to 'individualism' and to 'liberal' learned societies and academies, until the beginning of the nineteenth century when, with the foundation of the

University of Berlin, and later University College in London, universities once again became the seats of higher education and the home of living culture and science.

We are now living through a fresh period of transition. Schools in general and universities in particular often remain attached to 'traditional values', partly because the teaching staff have grown old – in mind even more than in years – and are therefore incapable of keeping up with the times, but have settled into a dogmatic, individualistic, academic and humanistic view of culture; and also because, now that they are part of the State and its Establishment they share its inertia. In every composite society there exists a cultural lag such that some groups, institutions, organisations, generations and individuals remain straggling behind, clinging to accepted values and incapable of further evolution, while other groups, organisations, institutions, generations and individuals opt for 'emergent values'.[63] The superstructure of the State, except when the State is itself emergent and revolutionary, usually takes upon itself to defend the Conservative values providing the reason – or pretext – for its continuation in power, whereas the universities and schools in general naturally tend to take different lines. Their bureaucratic and administrative elements are more dependent on the State organisation – on the Ministry of Education in European countries – and so make common cause with it. When a crisis overtakes the State organisation itself, the State disclaims any openly political attitude and declares that the universities should be *isolated* from society, and provide an education that, while not militantly defending traditional values such as scholasticism, classical humanism and academicism, is at least politically and socially aseptic, shut off from the external world, and dedicated to the transmission of learning without contact with the realities of a society in transition. In such cases as this, only the most youthful in spirit among the teaching staff, and the active and militant members of the student body, try to keep communication open between school and society, and confront 'traditional values' with 'emergent values'. But a society as a whole, or its more powerful majority, may be self-satisfied and conformist. Then the more dynamic elements in the universities, isolated and impotent, try to convert the universities into a 'refuge for individualists', as Riesman explains, and live in hopes of better days (non-conformity serving the ends of better communication). When, instead of coming to terms with a stagnant State organisation and a conformist society possessing the government it deserves, a revolutionary group with too 'ideological' a view of culture[64] seizes power, the schools are converted into organs of indoctrination, rather than of critical, analytical and rational teaching, driving from their last refuge Riesman's 'individualists', who believe in communication between schools and society but also that culture cannot be reduced to terms of politics.

Where there are different cultural institutions and groups within the same society, some representing new attitudes of mind, new hopes and new values, while others are retarded and reactionary, keep to the old ways of life and defend tradition against innovation, the young people in schools and universities, eager for the latest knowledge, and the more enlightened teachers seem naturally to play the part of a cultural *avant-garde*, or pilot-plant to the society of the future, or a ferment which will set the whole community in motion when once communicated to the masses.

But this can only happen when the schools and universities are politically independent from the State. As has already been said, the university is an organ set up by society for the purpose of rigorous, methodical self-criticism, not because its immediate mission is social criticism, but because such criticism is implicit in the social analysis which is the object of the so-called 'humanities'. Does this scientific independence from politics and the State necessitate complete autonomy for the university? By no means. It would be a poor State indeed that could not bear criticism from its *own* university! The university has the right to full scientific and political independence but not to autonomy of organisation. The great era of free and private universities is now over, anyway in Europe. At a time when every country is going in for economic and social planning, how can the foundation of centres of learning be left to individual enterprise or to groups of private interests, however worthy? It is clear that the schools must be planned on strictly technical lines, in the interests of culture and its extension throughout the country, of economic development, and of the creation and maintenance of democracy. (Democracy always involves a continuous struggle to maintain itself.) The opposite error would be for the *planning* of the university to be rigorously imposed from above, and its *organisation* left in the hands of the Ministry, without reference to teaching and student bodies. Both must be established democratically, even though authoritatively; they must always avoid dogmatism, and remain accessible to whatever adjustments experience and the wishes of those involved may prove necessary.

At this point we must pause and contrast the organising (or executive) with the academic (or university) spirit. Although I write as a university man who does not hold, nor ever has held, any executive power whatever, I must admit that the view of the academic, aristocratic minority that a professorship is a 'liberal' vocation, entitling its owner to be treated with respect and to impart a 'magisterial', abstract and inefficient education, is sufficiently often an obstacle to real scientific and technological development.[65] The remedy is not to be found in organised technocracy, however, but on one hand in the 'continuous education' of teachers (as of all modern men: see the last chapter) through new knowledge, discoveries and inventions, through the needs and aims of society, and through their own pupils; and on the other hand by the introduction into the organisation of schools and universities of a *dynamic* element, which, without going to the extremes found in some Latin-American countries, can be contributed only by the students and the younger members of the teaching staff. A share in the government of their school or the administration of their university must be given to students, as discreetly and gradually as is thought prudent so long as it is not purely symbolical but effective and real, so that schools and universities can provide an education for democracy as well as an education that is democratic, scientific, technological, professional and morally formative.

This leads us to our third problem, concerning communication inside the universities and schools, which could be considered from the same point of view as the last – administration, instruction, research and social services.[66] I propose however to investigate communication between the teaching staff and the students, not only with reference to personal relationships but also to communication of the educational message and identification with school or university.

As to the first of these, the climate in the classrooms or lecture-rooms of a school may be authoritarian or democratic.[67] The reciprocal attitude between teachers and students influences the results of one or other method of communication: there may be well-disciplined classes, spontaneously accepting their teacher's prestige, or student groups may express a youthful subculture and come into conflict with their schoolmasters; classes may accept their teacher as their natural leader[68] and be eager to work under his guidance and share his views of the world, or have their own organisation and want to be taught what interests them rather than what their teacher chooses (it may be the same course he has been going over for years and years). A teacher's adaptability and goodwill may be shown by quick and direct communication, by his accessibility and readiness to give any information he can, to direct studies, make suggestions, give advice and do research with his pupils. Or he may reveal his total unsuitability to his task by carrying out his duties in a purely formal way, and inhibiting or cutting short communication with his pupils by his 'formality' and remoteness.[69] It is clearly becoming increasingly difficult for a teacher solemnly to impart culture to his pupils, while they meekly absorb the behaviour-patterns dictated to them. However discreetly and implicitly, the students demand that their hopes, interests and objectives should be taken into account, as well as their own subculture – which is so important for communication and socialisation among themselves and to the functional structure of their peer-group, as studied by Riesman and other educational sociologists. When teachers are well-disposed to this subculture, education takes two directions[70] – from pupil to teacher and from teacher to pupil – and results in the 'continuous education' of the teaching staff, as has already been suggested and will be elaborated in our last chapter.

The content of the educational message has been decoded and explained, both intellectually and factually, in a penetrating study by P. Bourdieu and J. C. Passeron.[71] Their central hypothesis, now in process of further empirical verification, is that the 'language of ideas' used by a teacher as a perfectly 'natural' means of communication, is a pure fiction: the teacher's language has to be 'deciphered', and most of the students are incapable of doing this correctly. The pupils only half understand, as they would an imperfectly mastered foreign language, but the undergraduate habit of listening to professional jargon, course after course and year after year, gives them a feeling of familiarity with it, so that they understand enough to manipulate the language themselves. After all, all they need do is put together terms they have heard thousands of times associated by their teacher and which appear in the same contexts in the books they have been advised to read, though there is some probability of their talking nonsense, or at least saying things that have more apparent than real intellectual content. The result is that the educational message, thus transmitted in dogmatic, condensed and possibly brilliant lessons, is useful to a very small minority, who are capable of following their teacher step by step, and absorbing a large amount of information in the shortest possible time without unnecessary explanations. But it is only very slightly useful to the mass of the student population, who not only fail to understand, but – what is much worse – make a habit of using 'ritual' language which actually means almost nothing to them. Thus by a sort of 'verbal reflex' they deceive themselves into believing that they are moving in an atmosphere of true university culture. (The typically French phenomenon of a *canular*, is a not very exaggerated caricature of this almost purely 'verbal' form of pseudo-communication, in which words are linked together because they belong to the same type of vocabulary, 'intellectual' jargon or terminology, rather than in order to express an idea.)

If this is what happens in the sphere of intellectual understanding, it is no better when facts have to be absorbed. The teacher may be talking about classical literature, for example, or the golden age of the drama, but most of the students are unable to respond to the literary or artistic message of these ancient works, and find them as remote from their own sensibilities and way of life as they are far away in time. As for the intellectual approach, it comes up against the obstacles we referred to in the last paragraph.

Why should such a state of things be allowed to continue? Paradoxically enough – this is the conclusion our two authors come to – there is a tacit agreement between both parties to preserve a situation that so conveniently reduces communication to a minimum. Since teachers and students belong to totally different worlds and subcultures, why try to establish genuine and thorough communication, which is obviously doomed to failure? In the teacher's view, his remote contact with the students comes to an end with his monologue, while the students listen, shrouded in the anonymity of the lecture-hall, feeling exempt from any need to participate and confident that they will be 'left in peace'. This reciprocal remoteness allows the teacher to speak exclusively about what he has prepared in advance, without any danger of being attacked by 'awkward' questions or objections. And the student knows that if he remains passive he will keep his independence and not be bothered with embarrassing interrogations which would destroy his self-deception of 'having understood' the lesson. This fictitious communication means that neither teachers nor students need devote themselves *entirely* to education, and the university is to them both rather a phase to be completed than something they should dedicate themselves to wholly.

Obviously this acute analysis of the roles of teacher and student is not universally applicable. In France, teaching takes place in large amphitheatres and traditionally consists in lectures; it is completely different from the predominantly practical and technological[72] education given informally to small groups – some have been described as 'cafeteria-style' – in American universities. The book on *Educational Research* referred to above[55] presupposes the special structure and organisation of American universities and institutes, and their new perspectives cannot easily be translated into terms of other educational and research organisations. Hence the importance of a comparative sociology of education, starting from the outlook adopted in the present book and attempting to establish *communication* between the educational systems of different countries.

A final subject remains to be dealt with: that of *identification* with the school or university. A difficult question today. In the past, the great universities – Oxford and Cambridge, the Sorbonne and Montpellier, Salamanca and Alcalá – each had its own individual style and way of life. During periods of traditional culture the young integrated themselves easily and completely with 'their' school, and felt what might be called by analogy intellectual patriotism for their university (their *Alma Mater*). Today things have changed. For one thing the teaching staff have lost social status, largely because they are so poorly paid; in some countries they cannot live decently on their salaries, in others these are totally inadequate, and they are always less than the earnings from other professions needing much less preparation. For another thing, the community has accepted the stereotyped view that a university don lives isolated from adult life, mixing only with the young, and is generally either eccentric or frustrated.[73] But, as we have seen, the dealings most teachers have

Graduation day at a large American university. With such over-population, the contact between teacher and student must be remote; other pressures work against identification with a specific academic atmosphere or environment. Instead there may be more concern for the subject as a chosen professional field.

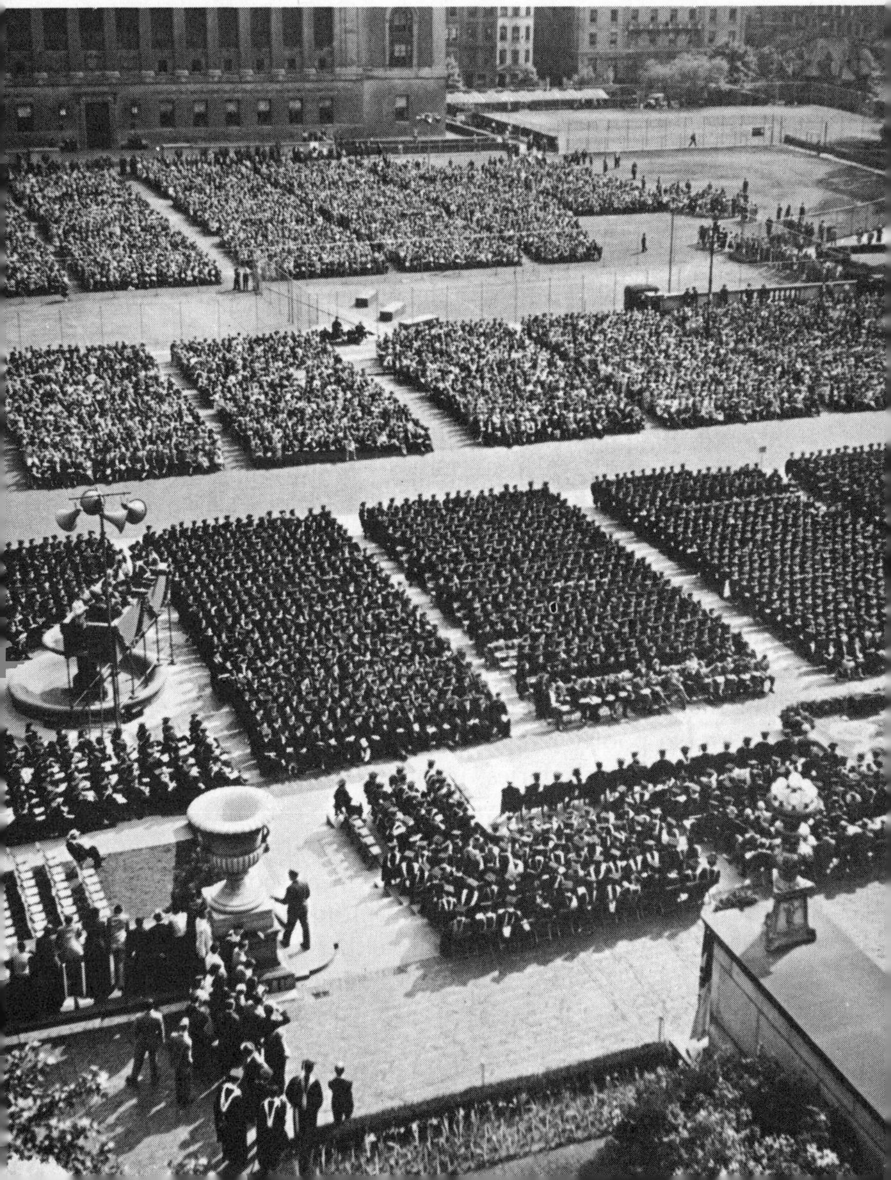

with the young are becoming progressively more difficult and strained, for the young have lost their old respect for them, and no real closeness of approach or better understanding has come to take its place. Nor do the students identify themselves with their aristocratic colleges and universities as in the past. Social discrimination between universities is dwindling, and a backward student, or one who simply wants to become independent from his family, finds he has to work too hard to have time for full identification with his university.[74] But this subject has received considerable attention from contemporary American educational sociologists.[75] We must distinguish between identification with the university and with the faculty or department; and also between scholastic and professional orientation.[76] But such distinctions are too specialised to be gone into in detail here.

23 Aesthetic or artistic communication

In Part One we studied the special characteristics of artistic communication. We also found that, contrary to what is often believed, understanding of the aesthetic message requires education of a very special sort, fundamentally consisting in opening any channels of communication that are blocked by clichés, by conventional, established, traditional or 'kitsch' art, or by a tendency to enjoy works because they are in keeping with established fashions or standards, and to decipher them with a ready-made 'key'. Whereas the truth is that modern art cannot be unlocked by keys, but only by readiness to respond freely and be 'impressed' by it.

A free art, which has no 'keys' and is self-explanatory, is essentially art of *Einmaligkeit*[77] as Walter Benjamin called it, in other words always unrepeatable and unique, never academic. Yet, in fact, as soon as an authentic work of art has been produced, its secret is turned into a 'formula' or 'recipe' and exploited by imitators; sometimes even the artist himself cultivates his own mannerisms and dedicates himself to self-plagiarism. But this cannot happen until the new art has opened its channels of communication. Until this moment, it has to struggle, as Norbert Wiener saw, to overcome the barrier interposed by the storehouse of artistic information which already bears the seal of approval and bars the way to any discordant aesthetic message. Thus a new work of art may be caught between the Scylla of non-reception and the Charybdis of commercial exploitation when the channels of acceptance by impresarios, picture-dealers or publishers are at last opened, either by the artist himself, or by unskilled imitators or much improved new methods of

BATTLE OF HASTINGS
1066
BOTTLE OF GUINNESS
1966
GUINNESS

reproduction – a completely modern development noticed by Walter Benjamin.

And so we are inevitably faced with the problem set by Benjamin[78] of the relation of art to the masses, which is inseparable from the strictly aesthetic problem of the relation between a work of art's 'capacity for information' and 'capacity for complexity' – to use Moles's expressions. The less information a work of art has to offer – that is to say the less new it is – the more easily it is accepted by the masses, and if it can avoid the danger of too slight 'complexity' and therefore of apparent triviality, it will have a good chance of 'success'. Moreover, a truly aesthetic receptor can 'lose himself', become submerged in an artistic message surcharged with information, and bide his time; but this is only possible to the humble élite – or, in his own way, to an intellectual snob. When on the contrary the new art is accepted, largely thanks to its imitators, and people get accustomed to it, it soon gets commercialised and multiplied to a fabulous extent by technical reproduction. At the same time a true work of art may be 'degraded', as happened when the *Gioconda* was used for advertising purposes, or some famous Madonna reproduced a hundred times till she degenerated into *bondieuserie*.[79] The reverse process may also occur: objects that have no artistic value whatever, or – even worse – are in bad taste, may be deeply penetrated with reality, as in Van Gogh's painting of old boots whose significance was explained by Heidegger. Or else, a more modern phenomenon noticed by Gillo Dorfles, they may be salvaged and combined together; we see examples of this in the sophisticated use of some ordinary illustration, the incorporation of non-aesthetic materials in informal art, and 'pop-art'.

As soon as one begins to understand it, this ebb and flow, this ephemeral quality, this fugacity of modern art, its oscillation between pure aesthetic value and realism, while they give it a special semantic value, do not seem capricious or casual. The artist is responding to the rhythm of modern life, revealing its profundities, unwittingly denouncing it while at the same time embracing it as his destiny. No sociology of artistic communication[80] can ignore this transience, this ineluctable desire to 'linger behind' and at the same time be 'with it', which are the most obvious qualities

Van Gogh's *Boots*. 'Objects that have no intrinsic value whatever . . . may be deeply penetrated with reality'.

of the fleeting, contemporary yet historical, works of art of our speeded-up vital tempo.

Thus the aesthetic experiences of the élite and the masses naturally come into conflict. Mass-produced art neither is nor ever will be art in the true, fastidious and valid sense of the

Pop art: Jim Dine's
Walking Dream with a 4-foot Clamp.

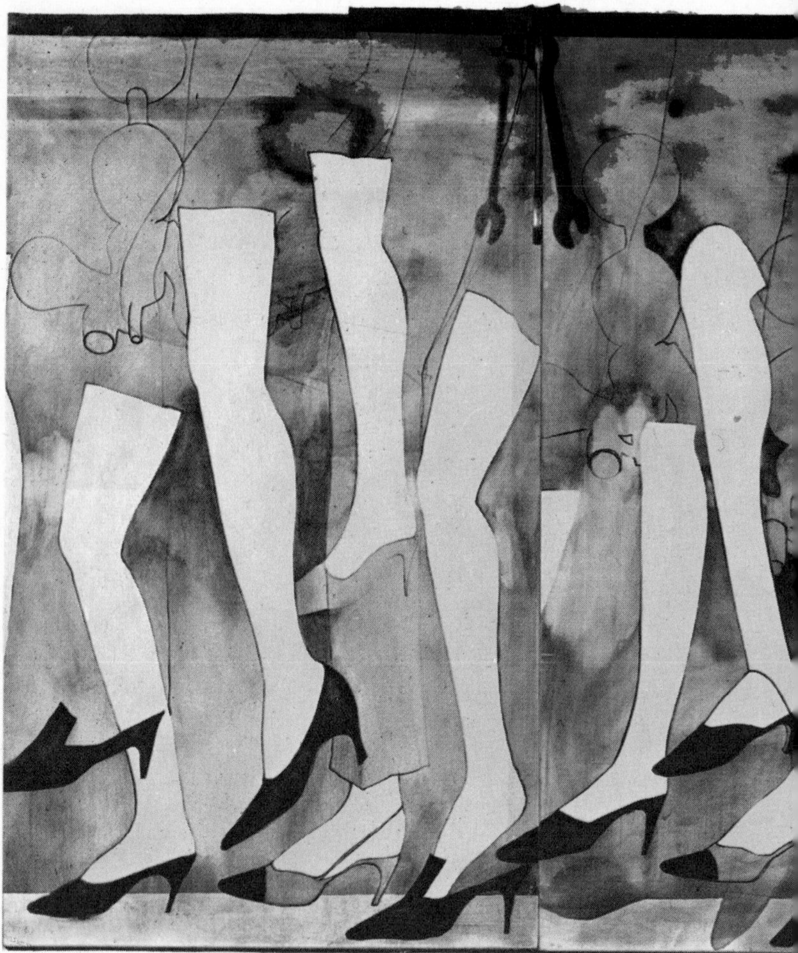

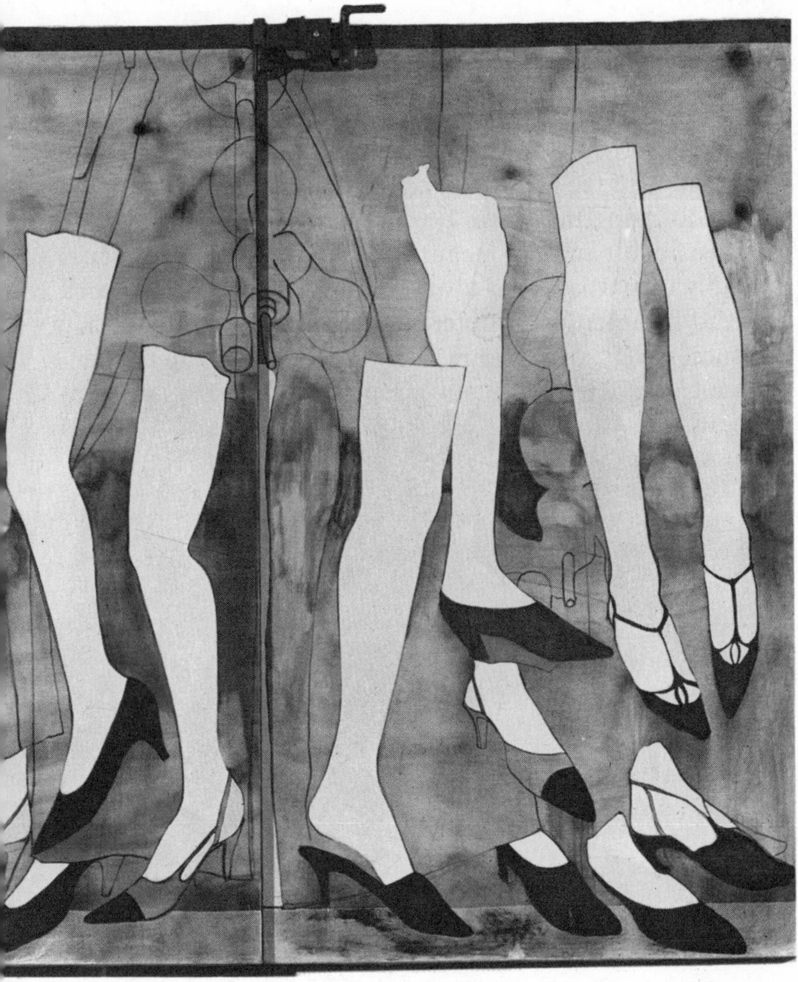

word. Nevertheless, most of the authentic aesthetic experiences of our contemporaries are produced by this (pseudo) art. Our problem has thus led to a wider one: whether it is desirable, not only for art but for all our culture, to be integrated with the life of the masses and to take into account the conditioning they have been subjected to, the quality of their sensibility and the means of arousing it. The answer is probably now what it has always been: a truly classical work can emit information at different levels, both simultaneously and successively, or, in simpler terms, it can speak to *all* men, although it does not by any means say *the same thing* to them all.

24 Socio-economic communication

Until now 'communication' has been understood in this book to mean 'language' in the broadest sense of the word. But, as Lévi-Strauss has observed, social communication is not concerned merely with messages, but also with women and wealth. Now it is precisely these two last forms of communication that determine the socio-economic structure of groups. The practice of endogamy and the restriction of wealth to a caste or subgroup both lead to a static and closed society. Positive rules concerning marriage and parental relationships belong to primitive societies with rigid social customs. Modern societies only accept negative or prohibitive rules against incest, marriage with someone of a different caste, means, social class or race (especially with negroes in the United States not to mention South Africa). But there are degrees of prohibition. An incestuous marriage is finally excluded, whereas the other forms of communication of women are tending to become easier, and to be at most 'thought ill of' socially; they may, and indeed often do, lead to *déclassement*, but are not now formally forbidden.

In primitive societies there is a close relation between communication of women and communication of wealth, and this persists to some extent in modern society; access to a higher social class may be gained through marriage (a movement in the opposite direction to *déclassement*) or by fortune-hunting, etc. But Western society is no longer organised feudally or according to ownership of land, but by big business and capitalism; this means that its wealth is not *present*, *tangible* and *limited*, and therefore that marriage is no longer the chief means of getting into a superior class, though it may sanctify and give social recognition to such an economic ascent. Modern man does not possess, accumulate and hoard his wealth, he *makes* it by exploiting the world's resources, which big business and technology have taught him to extract from it. The problem thus does not depend on communication or incommunicability of women, as in primitive societies, but on communication or incommunicability of wealth, naturally of *productive* wealth. When the acquisition of political power by the bourgeoisie and the first industrial revolution led to the creation of a capitalist society, wealth remained in the hands of a few of the owners of industry; with the ending of the old guild system and the exodus from the country to the great industrial cities, everyone else – or at least the vast majority of the population – was sooner or later reduced, or condemned, to swell the enormous, defenceless army of the proletariat. A rigid, unsurmountable barrier inevitably developed between the subgroups or social classes, somewhat like that of primitive societies, but resulting from the incommunicability of productive wealth – not of women. This, as is well known, is how Marx saw capitalist society, a view whose next and equally unavoidable phase was to be the revolution of that vast proletariat, who would dethrone the bourgeoisie, seize power and institute its own dictatorship. Marx's prophecy has been partly *self-fulfilling* and partly *self-defeating*. He succeeded in making the proletariat class-conscious, and in mobilising them for the struggle; and in some countries (not the most industrialised as he thought, but the reverse) his ideas have been victorious. On the other hand he helped correct the errors of a too rapacious capitalism by giving rise to a development he could never have imagined – a new, tertiary class of occupation having nothing to do with the proletariat. Meanwhile the proletariat changed its character, became diversified, and lost its previous unity. Finally consumption on what had been until quite recently considered a lavish scale was made accessible to the workers themselves, thereby opening a new home market. Thus reformed, neo-capitalist society tends to see itself in terms of a social 'ladder', which can be ascended or descended with the help of energy, industry, study, enterprise and intelligence, rather than as made up of stratified layers (the social classes) one on top of the other, that are unable to mix or communicate. Contemporary society is not divided into classes, but forms a *continuum*, and the place of any individual in it is a matter of *status*, chiefly depending – by a paradox showing the unavowed materialism of the West – on the size of his income. It depends on income or annual earnings, for wealth in the old tangible sense – of land, and later on factories – does not in fact now belong to *individuals*. Anonymous societies, the only possible means of collecting the huge capital needed today, have rendered invisible the great and 'heroic' (in spite of their inhumanity) capitalist financiers of the past. The formulas of so-called popular capitalism and of technocracy in the field of business management have completely depersonalised industry in the eyes of the masses, who know the names of a great many film stars and singers and of some great writers, but of very few business men.

The ordinary Marxist, tired of dogmatism and mental laziness, tends to see this profound but over-rapid change as a mere 'manipulation of the masses' – a capitalist device by which class society has been replaced by an amorphous and fragmented society of the masses. But like all moralistic explanations based on the perfidy or 'cunning' of the few, this is obviously not a very convincing argument. We must try and get a little closer to the facts.

We saw that until the beginning of the technological age the great inventors were very rarely men of science, but technicians in the old style, or skilled artisans; in just the same way industrialists used to have no special knowledge: it was enough if they had the 'spirit of enterprise'. Today things have changed, and technology has become indispensable for business management as well as for invention. The principal role in a business is not played by the owner, but by the director, manager or chief executive, the man who takes responsibility and makes decisions. Whether the business is really owned by a group of rich old men of the 'leisured classes', a few artists who have been successful and invested their savings, or a great many humble shareholders, is of little importance. The man who takes decisions is the one who matters. Decision-making is just as vital to the economics of industry as it is to politics. But it is becoming less possible to make decisions in an arbitrary way; they must be rational. A *science of decision-making* is evolving today, based on the sciences of information and communication.* The position of an *industrial democracy* is parallel to

* A new book on this subject is Arnold Kaufmann's *The Science of Decision-making* (World University Library).

that of a *political democracy*. Its problems cannot be solved by diluting responsibility or by putting decisions to the vote. There must be some responsible individual with 'executive power' and 'power to make decisions'. But in order that he should function in a democratic and rational way, and not as a dictator, he must be well-versed in technology and keep himself constantly informed, so that even the least important channels of communication are always open, and partnership in the management of the business is complete. From this it follows that pedagogic communication, or education, is an indispensable element of real and effective partnership in industrial management, and we shall show that the same holds good of political organisation.[81]

25 Political communication

With political communication we return again to the field with which so much of this book has been concerned – the transmission of messages – language in the widest sense of the word, including, as we saw at the end of Part One, extra-linguistic semantic elements: gestures (like the Communist salute with raised fist, the Fascist salute in the style of ancient Rome, Churchill's V-sign during the war); secularised rites and ceremonies; musical and mixed elements (military marches, national, revolutionary and Fascist anthems).

Language in the strictest sense changes with changing political situations. Compare for example two political languages, both eminently rhetorical: the literary, humanistic and often humanitarian language of nineteenth-century politicians on the one hand, and on the other Mussolini's trenchant, super-human rhetoric (a cross between Nietzsche and Sorel), d'Annunzio's 'literary and decadent' apologia for war, and Marinetti's 'futuristic' version – 'war is beautiful because it has led to the human body becoming metallised as in some fantastic dream'. Compare the religious and theological language used by governments of past centuries and their anachronistic imitators with the mythical, eschatological, messianic and revivalist language of revolutionary politicians of the extreme left, or with Hitler's equally mythical speeches, full of irrational near-hysterical vitality. Notice again the modern taste for political speeches derived from science and technology (Harold Wilson, Kennedy's 'Brainstrust', and G. Defferre); and also the tendency of present-day governments towards a sober concrete precision in communication.

But so far we have only dealt with communication in a single direction – from governor (or governors) to the governed. This one-way traffic is in fact the fundamental characteristic of anti-democratic régimes, expressed in terms of the theory of information.

It may be inferred from what has been said about the oratorical styles of Mussolini and Hitler that the totalitarian leaders did not set out to 'inform' in the very least, but merely to impose their point of view with the help of a skilful mixture of emotive persuasion and threats, coloured with frenzied, nationalist – or racist – exaltation. Instead therefore of any real information, it was a case of unilateral communication, after which decisions were taken on irrational grounds (Carl Schmitt's 'decisionism'). This form of politics amounts to 'decision for decision's sake', 'communicated' in such a way that those who were subjected to it accepted it, either because they were carried away by exaltation and emotional tension, or under the influence of terror.[82]

This monopoly of channels of communication from above downwards makes it easy to manipulate the (pseudo) opinion of the public; all mass-communication media are purely and exclusively at the service of the government.[83] However, even in régimes having no recognised channels of communication from below upwards, messages can obviously be received either from abroad or from dissentient individuals with enough personality, prestige or civic importance to try and make their voices heard. But these messages are immediately intercepted for example by suppressing the circulation of foreign newspapers transmitting unwelcome information.

Or at least everything possible is done to intercept them: interference and 'noise' make telecommunication difficult, and at times severe restrictions are imposed, such as penalties for those who listen to foreign radios and pass on foreign news. Thus only a few can express an opinion: only one, to be precise, for the others merely echo him. The vast majority of subjects (subjects, not citizens) have no choice but to receive this opinion passively, for communication has been so organised that response of any sort is impossible or inaudible. Communication from the governed to their administrators may eventually be almost completely cut off.

But we must not think that a purely formal opening of the channels of communication is enough to produce true democracy. In our second case of interruption for example the confusion may be caused by anarchic elements among the governed. Again, the media of information, though apparently facilitated and controlled by the State, may in fact be monopolised by high finance, which may have no interest in totalitarianism or dictatorship but certainly has none in full and authentic democracy. 'Free enterprise is not liberty', writes Duverger, 'above all because it depends on money. The media of communication are free from the State, but not from money.'[84] And money is essentially Conservative. Naturally the means used by a Conservative plutocracy to obstruct true democratisation are more subtle than those of pure authoritarianism. The man who wants to read or hear about real problems is distracted by trivial news items and advertisements, descriptions of weddings or the lives of film-stars, sensational events, famous love-affairs and crimes of passion, the doings of members of 'café society' and so forth, which produce laziness, apathy and indifference to politics, and that 'depolitisation' which always in fact amounts to conformist acceptance of the established régime. Is this use of mass media deliberate or not? We must return here to what has been said about information for publicity purposes; but instead of mere repetition, let us quote Maurice Duverger's very fair evaluation of the situation:

The Communists declare that this procedure is intentional, that the capitalists deliberately make use of 'romances', stories about Princess Margaret, sporting and cinema adventures, so as to make the masses forget how they are being exploited, and sterilise their desire to rebel. Objectively, the information of liberal régimes is tending to this result. Subjectively, it does not seem to spring from any conscious process or deliberate intention, but from the mechanism of gaining custom.[85]

Democratisation therefore above all depends on the desire for partnership; it is a question of politisation or re-politisation. If this were achieved in a formally democratic régime with universal suffrage, political changes would follow the will of the majority. The necessary channels would be provided, and mass media would give clients what they asked for – in this case politics. But politics must no longer be a matter for over-subtle argument between professionals. Parliamentarism, as well as causing obstruction by its incompetence and love of discussion for discussion's sake, hinders executive efficiency in the scientific technology of taking decisions (a subject that will be dealt with shortly), and provides a very inadequate channel of communication for the governed from our present point of view. Members of parliament soon form a closed circle. They turn their backs on the real state of the country and are interested only in remaining in power and distinguishing themselves. Our epoch can lay claim to other more effective channels for question and answer, and for lively, open, technical, discussions between the professions and unions and those in power. Although 'direct democracy', strictly speaking, is at present impossible, and political parties, lightened of the burden they carried in the nineteenth century, are still indispensable for the task of politisation or re-politisation referred to above, it is essential that politics should stop being 'discussion' – not in order to rush into pure 'action', but so as to develop on a basis of political science. Here we again come up against the fact that political communication, like all other types, depends upon pedagogic communication, in the present case on 'political education'. Clubs for the study of politics – so important in present-day France – are probably the best means for this concrete re-politisation of the old parties and parliaments, so that they become suitable instruments for discussion between the active and influential sections of the population and the executive, which, as all the world agrees today, must be safeguarded against parliamentarism.

Decisions do in fact have to be taken by the executive. But they must not be made on irrational grounds, as in totalitarian 'decisionism', nor yet by a technocracy. Technocracy, apart from the fact that it is an illusion (because politics and political ethics cannot be eliminated) and a new form of tyranny, is a bad system of government from the technical point of view of cybernetics and the theory of information. Decisions taken by a government should never be rigid; they must be subject to self-correction according to new information. Future conduct should be supported by and readjusted according to the effect of an executive decision on events and the people governed. A rigid or authoritarian form of government denies itself this advantage of getting support from past events, of altering course, of flexibility and adaptation to the experience of those governed, or those occupying inferior government positions. If we picture society as a single great animal organism, we shall understand the folly of trying to govern its behaviour from the brain according to a pre-established plan, without also taking into account, or even receiving, sensorial communications about surrounding dangers and the new possibilities provided by a changing situation.

Government is basically conceived today in terms of planning, that is to say with a view to the future, as has been said of communication in general from the beginning of this book. But this planning or foresight must, in the first place, be carried out democratically, which does not mean that it must be adopted by everyone at the same time, but that all must take an active part so as to feel they 'belong' and are 'committed to it', as they cannot if it is imposed from above. Secondly it must be flexible though firm, ready to adapt itself to fresh information and learn (when will governments understand how much they have to learn!), according to the model, not of seventeenth-century mechanics and its automata, but of cybernetics, and projectiles that are self-directed towards their destinations, that move 'freely' (as we should anthropomorphically describe it) rather than by remote control. Finally all this necessitates the greatest possible development of the network of political communications, and constant attention to them. Only on the basis of the *science of information* can a real *science of decision* be founded, so as to co-ordinate information systematically and prevent decisions being imposed on social reality, and on human reality, and doing them violence or mechanising them. As Wiener has said, we are not frightened of machines but of the men in control of them. And here we must make one more appeal to the morality and democratic feeling of men of science.

Moreover, communication by the most expensive mass media, such as radio and television, must be guaranteed to all; these media should be nationally owned and organised as public services available to those of all shades of opinion.

26 International and oecumenical communication

Until quite recently when one spoke of communication, or rather of communications in the plural, one was understood to be referring to means of locomotion, roads and the vehicles using them, railways, ships; and it used to be said of a place that its communications were 'good' or 'bad'. Obviously the network of communications in this sense of locomotion (which is not incompatible with the other, for messages circulate by road and the post by railway, ships and air) has developed enormously, and will still develop very much more, especially in the air. This of course has effectively conduced to easier travel, in fact to improved international communication. Communication of women – marriages between young people of different nationalities – and communication of wealth – the post-war Marshall Plan and economic assistance to underdeveloped countries – have been important contributions to a closer understanding and solidarity between nations. Naturally this last form of communication involves the danger of a relapse into colonialism – this time in economic form; as also happens in the former case, when 'human material' is imported into a country, in a sort of neo-slavery, to do rough, unskilled jobs that the inhabitants do not want to do themselves.

But these media of communication must not make us forget the chief subject of our study: men of different nations can today communicate with ease without moving from home. This, like the speed of modern travel, has diminished the importance of the diplomatic corps of the past, and should contribute to direct understanding between nations.

The establishment of permanent bodies for communication – the old League of Nations and the present United Nations, as well as others of smaller scope – is something we must continue to fight for tirelessly and at all costs, in spite of apparent failure. Communications must never be cut, not even with those who appear to be enemies.

Apart from these planned unions – the United Nations, the Common Market and so on – there exists today as in the past a polymorphic structure of international alliances, which is never completely stable, for the world pattern is an essentially changing one. However, it is vitally important to keep the conversation going, not only within the various blocs and their subsystems but also between the blocs themselves.[86]

These blocs seem to be divided by their different political ideologies, and by conventional mythologies that impose an image of the enemy which often bears very little relation to the facts. What is therefore needed is continuous international communication on the one hand, and on the other a strictly objective analysis of the circumstances and inner meaning of the situation, so as to cancel the superficial, hasty and over-simple pictures by which the 'ideologies' of both right and left try to synthetise and sum it up. The world is not divided into two Manichaean camps – the Good and the Bad. It is not a question of a Utopian attempt to do without ideologies, but of reducing the distance between analysis and synthesis, of creating an ideology that is serious and functional, and acts more as a structural model to increase understanding and help us modify reality than as intangible dogma.

Ideologies are economic as well as political. The character that socialism is acquiring in Europe helps one realise that 'capitalism' and 'Marxism' have become abstractions, whose effective significance is changing. Planning and some degree of nationalisation or socialisation is progressively on the increase in the countries of the West. And we see socialism as the most effective form of economic organisation for the development of backward countries rather than as a Marxist *Weltanschauung* or metaphysics. To help spread information about all these matters is to render a great service to international communication.

Communication is also an important means of destroying the mythical images that form barriers between races and prevent mutual understanding. The people of other countries are men like ourselves, and their administrators are not very different from ours. (It is in different systems of government that the vital distinctions occur.) Research into cross-cultures and a more objective and less nationalist approach to the teaching of history, have helped dissolve stereotyped images created abroad or deliberately fabricated by image-makers,[87] and so make a valuable contribution to information and international understanding. UNESCO has played a vital part in this.

According to Wiener, we have allowed a militarist way of thinking to impose itself; the Western nations show this in their attitude to Russia and China, but each country is looking at its own reflection in a mirror. The struggle against this menacing phantom leads to the invention of new technological and warlike artefacts, each more terrible than the last, and this 'apocalyptic spiral' can have no end.

The most effective means of preserving the difficult, precious and greatly threatened equilibrium called 'peace' is for all conflicts to be dealt with by world organisations maintaining permanent communication between countries, and for a firm adherence to pacts, negotiation and discussion.

In addition to international communication of a non-religious sort, there is a new development in the form of oecumenical communication. For centuries the churches and religions in general have lived in deadly enmity, even in the heart of the Christian world, where the split causing non-communication began with the Great Schism. The East broke off religious communication with the West, foreshadowing the political breach many centuries later. Some time afterwards, in the sixteenth century, non-communication (or excommunication in ecclesiastical language) entered the Western sphere of Christianity with Luther's Reform movement and its consequences. The next few centuries saw several attempts at discussion and communication, but the oecumenical movement – restricted from then on to the Protestant churches – did not take shape as such until the nineteenth century. This is not the place to consider it in detail, nor even to trace the different stages of the approach to oecumenism on the part of the Catholic church, which had espoused the Counter-reformation ever since the sixteenth century. The pontificates of John XXIII and Paul VI, the second Vatican Council, and Paul VI's journeys to Jerusalem and India, were unequivocal signs of the new attitude of open communication, not only with other Christian sects but also with non-Christian religions (witness the contemporary appreciation of Hindu spirituality on the part of important Catholics of the West), and even with irreligious world-philosophies by means of the channel opened by the encyclical *Pacem in Terris*, and organised by the *Paulus-Gesellschaft*. This is not of course the beginning of a movement of syncretism or even a vague form of eirenicon, but an attempt to unite those holding different religions and profane creeds by a close network of channels of communication such as has been outlined in the previous headings of this Part. For only through *communication* may true *communion* be some day achieved.

Part 4

Communication in the future

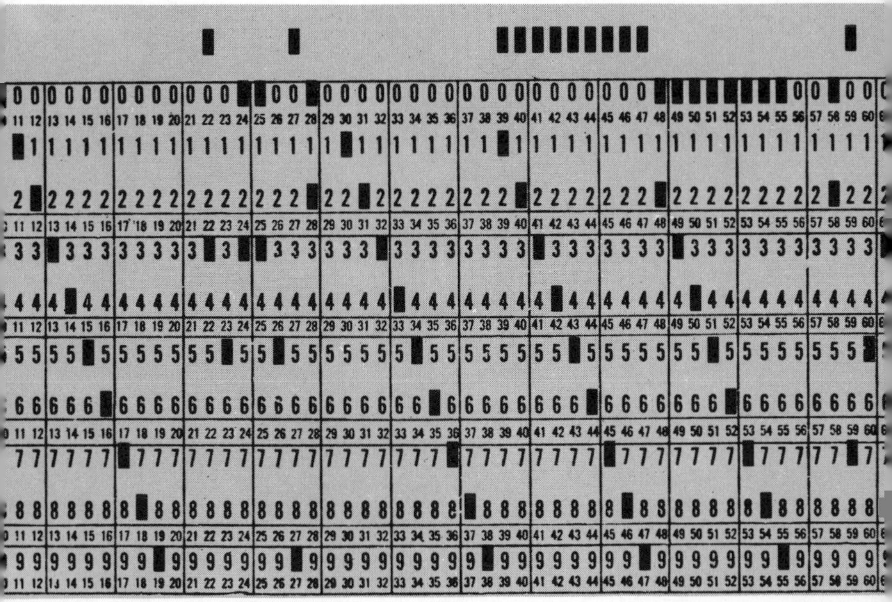

27 Prevision and decision for the future

It might almost be said that the basic thesis, explicit or implicit on every page of this book, is that all communication is anticipatory, purposeful, predictive and even normative. Communication always refers either to the future itself or to that imminently impending future we call the present. It is therefore not only natural but necessary that this book should end with an attempt to look straight at this future to which such constant allusion has been made.

The sense in which science can be understood as foresight – *savoir pour prévoir* – also takes us into the future. However, because modern science, unlike the contemplative *epistemê* of the ancients, can only be objectively understood through technology, through its effect on the world, and therefore presupposes prevision – *prévoir pour pourvoir* – it does not follow that *science* is actually the same thing as *prevision*, and certainly not that basic research can be reduced to applied science. As often happens in life, the attempt to get results quickly and directly is frustrated by impatience. Too great a hurry to acquire a lot of engineers and technicians, at the expense of apparently useless pure science, defeats its own end. And though, as we have shown, the purpose of science is its application, applied science is only possible because some fundamental research has previously been done, on which it must be based.

The sciences of prevision, if they deserve the name, are not like other sciences whose relation to the future is only latent and becomes apparent when they are applied. Instead they look directly to the future, explicitly predicting and forecasting it, not by intuition, prophecy and divination, but by rational means. The desire to foresee and dominate the future is essential to human nature. But in primitive races this took unscientific forms like divination and magic instead of the present-day sciences of prevision and decision.

These are still in process of being organised. To confine ourselves for the present to scientific prevision (we will deal afterwards with the sciences of decision), examples of such organisations known to me are: the Institute of Resources for the Future, established in Washington in 1952, and the Centre d'Études Prospectives, created by Gaston Berger, which periodically produces articles under the general title *Prospective* and a series called *Futuribles* edited by Bertrand de Jouvenel. There are of course a great many other individual and collective studies of the subject.[88]

The field in which this 'prospective attitude' – to use Gaston Berger's expression – has borne most fruit is of course economics, for, as Pierre Massé pointed out, no other human science is so subject to inertia, nor so easy to quantify statistically. It is therefore completely natural that it should serve as a pilot science, whose methods can be as far as possible adopted and/or adapted by the other social sciences that try to explore the future.

We are certainly heading towards a general theory of prevision and prediction today. The most serious risk involved – apart from those that belong to the sphere of science-fiction – is that of 'an over-simplification of history',[89] based on the implicit ethical premise that the chosen path is a privileged one, and the line we have taken is the only 'good', valid and correct one; whereas the truth is that only in an extremely limited sense can there be a high degree of probability that things will turn out 'as expected'. Hegel believed his own system to be the culmination of all philosophy; Marxist metaphysics claimed to have discovered the 'direction of history' from its beginning to its end; and (to take an example closer at hand) Julian Marias sees Ortega y Gasset as the point of convergence of the whole history of philosophy. Such macroscopic attempts to select *one* of the infinitely numerous threads from which history is woven, and use it as a guide-rope, are more to be admired for their confidence than for their rightness; they have let *decision* prevail over prevision, so as to simplify reality in accordance with their beliefs.

The characteristic note of present-day forecasting is that it tries to be rigorously scientific and not at all philosophical (either in the form of philosophy of history, or by projecting the past history of philosophy into the future). As was said before, science is not a synonym for prevision, and as Michael Polanyi wrote: 'prevision is not a necessary attribute of every scientific proposition'. Nonetheless science always to some extent anticipates observation; and just as history has been called prophecy in reverse, we are told by A. Marshall that 'explanation is simply prediction written backwards; and when fully achieved it helps toward prediction'.[90]

The point of departure for prevision and prediction[91] is the fact that our beliefs concerning a considerable part of future reality have a very high degree of probability. We do not start from zero when we forecast the future: there are a number of 'structural certainties' (Jouvenel) or 'stable factors' (Bell) that can be taken for granted unless totally improbable contingencies arise. That the sun will be rising and setting in three years time as it does today, that in two years time the British monarchy and the presidential regime of the United States will still exist, that in one year's time there will still be tension between the Western and Eastern blocs as well as within them both – these are permanent ingredients of historical reality, and it is reasonable to count on their persistence for an indefinite time, and their permanence from the point of view of the actual effects of our forecast. These examples show that the part of the future we assume to be certainly known consists in unstable as well as stable factors.

Within this 'frame' of the future there are other factors that can be calculated because they are susceptible to statistics and the laws of probability. These are changeable elements, but which follow a line of development – either upwards or downwards – that can be plotted with a high degree of probability by analysis of trends or the changing topology of present reality. What stage of evolution will the population of a certain country have reached in five years' time? How many people will have left the country for the town? How many programmers of cybernetic computors will England need in another three years? These are questions that can be answered with a reasonably small margin of error. There is also a part of reality that evolves rhythmically or cyclically instead of lineally. And another that changes very slowly: the laws governing its evolution may be unknown to us, but we can count on its 'resisting' the passage of time and not deteriorating easily. Even times of crisis and great historical revolutions can 'be seen coming' within wide and indefinite temporal limits; we feel that they 'had to happen'. All processes, according to Bell, contain hidden parameters that are not impossible to discover.

All these factors combine to make up a whole that is sufficiently difficult to determine with exactness because of the many independent variables involved; but of course history also presents us with a series of absolutely unforeseeable, fortuitous events. However, except in matters of pure chance, self-regulating, self-correcting prevision can foretell a great many imminent events, because an individual's capacity for movement is limited by his psychology and his situation, while the less agile movements of social groups and societies are limited by sociological laws; and natural 'movements' – except in the case of accidents like the death of a national leader from sudden illness – are nearly always predictable at short range. The description of the series *Futuribles* declares that 'each essay represents the author's own *views* (*vues*), and that since these views refer to what he thinks probable they must not be taken for the expression of his *desires* (*voeux*). But it is not always easy to draw this clear distinction between *vues* and *voeux*. A forecaster, however scientific he may be, is still a man with a man's prejudices, desires, preferences and values, which are bound to leave their mark and have some influence on his researches, whether he is aware of it or not. For instance, a research-worker who values scientific certainty above everything will cling to his structural concept and scorn as conjectural any events which refuse to fit into his pre-established scheme, whereas they may perhaps play a decisive part in world developments, and indicate a real revolution of some sort. Or, on the other hand, he may attribute exaggerated importance to merely superficial happenings, which can have no effect on the shape of things to come.

We have seen that modern science is not purely contemplative; it does not stand indifferently with arms folded predicting what is going to happen. On the contrary, when planning and science combine as a form of behaviour, they demand that man should intervene actively to alter events as he thinks 'best'. It is clear from this that the *sciences of prevision* can never be completely separated from the *sciences of decision.*[92] Gaston Berger said that '*l'avenir est affaire de volonté*'; Dennis Gabor called his famous book *Inventing the Future*, and G. L. Shackle described decision as the choice of a future goal through an act of creative imagination, rather than a choice between present advantages. The expression 'mathematical expectation' gives linguistic proof that the two levels are inseparable.

This does not imply any irrational 'decisionism', provided that the following three conditions are fulfilled. First, the sciences of decision must be based on the sciences of information in general, and in the present case particularly on those concerned with predicting or prevision (linear programming, theory of games, etc.). Secondly, since pure information and decision do not form a *continuum* and it is necessary to 'jump' deliberately from one to the other, this jump should be made in accordance with ethics and common-sense. Finally it follows that – unlike the neo-positivists – we must recognise the logical validity of value judgements and the ethical propositions formulating them – a subject that cannot of course be gone into here.

A decision should depend not only on previous information but also on its probable results, again to be predicted by means of information, as we saw in Part One. If a decision is to be rational, it must be supported, and even as it were surrounded, by information. Hence, as Gaston Berger clearly saw, rational decisions cannot be taken in isolation, as mere expedients to get out of a difficulty.

An administration must respond to the difficulties produced by changing reality, and invent solutions in advance – in fact it must convert itself into a science, the Science of Administration.[93]

28 On the danger that communication and man may become impoverished

The medium of communication *par excellence*, as we have repeated with tiresome frequency, is ordinary language. But, as some students of the sociology of culture have noticed, 'words are in retreat'. People talk less, and above all worse. We are witnessing a 'crisis in the language': it no longer serves to translate scientific communications, and it limps behind all the new artefacts with which modern man is surrounding himself, and which he can often only indicate (quite literally) by an abbreviation. As Ortega said, the objects out of which modern man constructs his life change so rapidly that the old quasi-magic association between word and thing is now unthinkable. We are even running to the opposite extreme. Reality, as modern man understands it, eludes language in two directions. Language has become too clumsy an instrument for men of science; yet for the man in the street it is too abstract, too unrelated to practical skills and the handling of all those appliances in daily use which have completely taken the place of nature as the frame for human lives.

There is no doubt that language is in a state of crisis today. But perhaps it is a crisis of growth? What seemed to us a few decades ago a model of style or wording, now appears rhetorical or conventional, slow and full of circumlocutions, or sometimes like a screen between us and reality, either making it difficult to see it or hiding it completely. I do not think it is pure chance that the *nouveau roman* has appeared in France, the country whose too 'polished' language needed it most. Rhetoric is like a crust, and if it is not removed it hinders contact with reality. And 'good' compositions and dissertations consist in skilfully threaded strings of 'general ideas' and thoughts (*pensées*) oscillating between topicality, brilliant but empty phrases and verbal paradox.

For ordinary spoken or written language to die is unthinkable. But we are certainly witnessing a radical reform tending to make it quicker and more agile, better adapted to the conditions of modern life. It seems to me that we have stopped speaking too well and now speak too badly. But I hope we are travelling towards a more desirable goal – a new, direct language, more closely connected with things themselves, more efficient, economical and flexible.

The rejection of rhetoric is one of the reasons – but there are many others – for the contemporary lack of interest in politics. Politics used to be almost exclusively a matter of 'fine words' as much for the leaders of the right ('sacred repository of tradition', 'defence of Western civilisation', 'fidelity to the greatness of our historic nation') as those of the left. The magic word 'liberty' is one of those that have been debased by use, probably because of the gap between its 'formal' and 'real' significance. Citizens have been replaced by consumers, as Sumberg realised,[94] and the best political system is simply the best economic one.

Now that modern man has ceased thinking of politics in terms of rhetoric, he sees it as a technique to be acquired like that of his own profession. Politics is becoming more and more a matter of administration and management of material interests, of planned expansion and development, all expressed in a jargon incomprehensible to the man in the street, and impossible to carry on without recourse to 'electronic

The videophone: probably not the ultimate promise (or threat) held by an audio-visual civilisation. Voice transmission being so cheap and picture transmission-lines so expensive, the videophone may not be widely introduced for some years.

brains' – to give them their popular name – and very difficult mathematical calculations. This 'apathy' towards political channels of communication is very easy to understand. How can one give an opinion about something one does not understand, and which is never explained to the members of pseudo-technocratic régimes? And again: perhaps this is because it is quite impossible for the uninitiated to understand it? There is no doubt that the technological details of the new politics, which is fundamentally economic, is very difficult for an uninitiated adult – though not for the young – to understand. But the basic issues on which an ethico-political decision always depends can be made intelligible to anybody. A few years ago it was the fashion[95] to describe politics in terms of lust for power, and speak of a technocratic neo-totalitarianism, visible in the very developments 'imposed' by the new technology: planning, automation, centralisation. Today we have again realised that tyranny cannot be produced by machines, but only enforced by the men who use them; that planning can be democratic; and that automation can be decentralised, as is happening at the moment, so that it becomes a network of channels with terminals in every small business, clinic or office, and in almost every private house. The problem of interest in public events is, as we have hinted before, one of political education, of re-politisation by way of new channels already being prepared and which will be facilitated by increased leisure time. Partnership in that great business, a nation, or in supra-national organisations, is a sober and serious matter, worthy of man's interest and enthusiasm – this is the sort of democracy to strive for.

It is sometimes predicted that the 'decadence of language' is leading us towards an *audio-visual civilisation*. Spoken language is in retreat because it is being replaced both by action and by formal languages, that is to say by signs and semiotics. And written language seems 'bookish' to modern sensibilities, and is being routed by the visual language of the cinema, television, illustrated magazines and comic strips. Books are increasingly invaded by illustrations, and – if they are scientific – by graphs, diagrams, extensive maps, tables,

A holiday-maker, comatose, gathers the necessary strength to photograph another succession of travel pictures. Only then, with everything 'done', will he be able to return to his work, which his holiday has copied faithfully in its alternation of rest and frenzied activity against the clock.

sociograms and organigrams. Modern man is being submerged in a world of largely but not entirely figurative images. We are heading towards a visual organisation of life as a whole. Even travel is tending to consist in a rapid succession of images, which naturally grow jumbled and confused in the memory as if one were quickly turning the pages of an illustrated book. And science fiction[96] is itself an attempt, completely in contrast with the essentially abstract spirit of modern science, to anticipate its technological results and visualise them in fantastic terms. Thus new inventions always arrive *late* with reference to the psychological *tempo* at which modern man is becoming accustomed to live; and laborious technological achievements seem to him easy and almost trivial because his capacity for surprise has been destroyed by the fantastic developments described by this type of literature – the dizzy journeys through space, discovery of forms of life preserved by centuries of hibernation, and a hundred other figments of the imagination based on the popularisation of relativistic physics. For everything is possible to the imagination and man enjoys becoming 'superman' for a while.

We referred just now to modern travel. The traveller of today divides his time between receiving a bewildering succession of visual impressions – afterwards virtually 'preserved'[97] in snapshots taken with the camera every good tourist carries – and spending whole days on end basking in the sun in quasi-vegetative tropism.

This alternation, like day and night or sleep and wakefulness, between relaxation[98] and the desire to lose no time and

Clover-leaf, multi-lane intersections which, when missed, cannot be found again are further aspects of modern communication difficult for the elderly to acquire. Quickness of visual thought and reflex is now part of the modern educational curriculum, as an important adjunct to intelligence and reasoning-power.

'miss nothing' – a sort of homeostatic regulation between tranquilisers and stimulants – makes up the life of modern man. Whether he is resting or subject to a series of conditioned reflexes, he sees his whole life increasingly controlled by a system of signs, like the electronically regulated traffic of a modern city. 'His whole life', I said advisedly, for his work, his free time, his needs and consumption (including culture), his sexual desires, his 'personal relations', and even his moral principles (a lubricant to make the wheels revolve more smoothly) are all coming under the control of systems of artificial, technologically produced signs.

What are we to think of this prophetic vision of human life, socialised and 'communicated' entirely through signs and images? As a tendency it is probably correct, but the picture is sometimes painted in too sombre colours.[99] Semiotic regulation is one of the consequences of rationalising the new needs created by the accelerated speed of life, the population explosion, the spread of urban life and all the demands it makes. Yet it is unjustifiably pessimistic to think that this increase of images and signs must necessarily impoverish human intelligence. It is not true that most users of the radio, cinema and television today have given up other subtler media of information; but rather that until recently only the most primitive and rudimentary media were available to them. Of course a poor understanding of history is got from so-called historical films; all the same they give people a simple picture of something they previously knew nothing at all about. We must not contrast the poverty of the culture transmitted by mass media with the richness, complexity and

variety of that available to the happy few – but with a total lack of it. And it would be wrong to suppose that understanding a sequence of images or an exact system of signs requires no intelligence. The intelligence needed in daily life today is a sort of visual thinking, difficult or impossible for the elderly to learn. One has only to take an old person to a film with a fast-moving plot, or drive with him along a motor-road at high speed, to realise that he either understands almost nothing, or else understands it too late, when the turning he wants us to take has been passed or new visual situations have complicated and changed the scene in which our 'slow' companion is still 'bogged down'.

It would be wiser therefore not to adopt either a pessimistic or a naively 'progressive' attitude to the world of the future, but to try and envisage it without hasty value-judgements, and guide it in the right 'direction'. As we have said throughout this book and especially in the present Part, it can be inferred that the civilisation of the future will be increasingly concrete, practical and audio-visual where the 'culture of the masses' is concerned. Technology or 'know how', is tending to get the better of 'know what'. In terms of useful behaviour a Copernican revolution is taking place analogous to the one Kant produced in the sphere of ethics: *how* we work is gaining primacy over *what* we make – what might be called the behaviourist and pragmatical *form* over the metaphysical *content*.

Unlike the culture of the masses, scientific culture is becoming more abstract and difficult to express in ordinary language, as well as less possible to represent by visual 'models'. This does not mean that it is moving further away from scientifically cognisable reality, but is like someone who steps back from an obstacle, takes a run at it, and so clears it more easily. Let us return for a moment to what was said in Part One about 'structure' and 'reality': by making abstract 'models' of reality we can reconstruct it intellectually and so understand it better.

If we want above all to understand and grasp reality, we must give primacy to the *sciences of reality* over the *normative sciences*, and of course over the *metaphysical sciences*. Thus political sociology, political science and the sociology of law[100] have progressed at the expense of the constitutional law of the past; the sociology and science of administration at the expense of administrative law; linguistics, the science of spoken language, at the expense of the old rules of grammar; the logic of ethics (the study of ethical terms and propositions) at the expense of ethics proper. This does not mean that a normative attitude has been abandoned – that would be impossible. But it has a new orientation: towards organisation, planning and the sciences of decision.

Of all the branches of knowledge studied today the future of the human race is most directly and profoundly affected by those applied to automation, to the use of atomic energy and to interplanetary communication (which will, for obvious reasons, not be dealt with here).

This is not the place to speak of the uses of atomic energy. It is enough to stress the fact that, as with automation, its peaceful uses – delayed by the development of the warlike ones – are tending to be directed, without prejudicing the great electric plants, towards smaller, more accessible, manageable appliances available to everyone. In other words it is moving in the direction of socialisation and democracy, and away from the terrifying mythical effulgence with which the armament-race has surrounded the atom (synonymous with the Bomb to the man in the street) or those mechanical supermen with vast electronic brains and fabulous powers of calculation, memory, order and organisation but no human feelings whatever, who have provided such abundant food for science-fiction. The social consequences of this 'democratisation' of the uses of atomic energy, particularly in the field of electronic 'information' or 'communcation', is of particular interest to our enquiry and will be dealt with in the next section.

Since they also fall under the heading of communication, although not strictly speaking communication of messages or information, something should perhaps be said here about the revolution in transport (locomotion) and urbanisation.

The congestion of motor-cars is producing increasingly serious transport problems. We seem to be trying to solve them by separating off different 'levels' of circulation for pedestrians and vehicles, and by creating different channels or whole routes for those by-passing and those entering a town, and motor-roads leading into and serving the different zones of great cities. More far-sighted predictions envisage moving pavements for pedestrians, and energy transmitted directly from networks on the surface of motor-roads to the vehicles travelling along them. Transport by air is often seriously delayed at take-off and landing, as anyone who has travelled by aeroplane in the United States knows from experience. Vertical or nearly vertical take-off and new methods of landing may solve this difficulty; meanwhile in the far distant future aeroplanes may receive energy for flight from high frequency networks covering the entire planet.

Urban communication or urbanisation is the subject of a new science; it forecasts urban deconcentration in the form of vast collections or 'nebulae' of towns linked together and covering hundreds of square miles, towns and whole regions being planned for touristic, industrial and agricultural exploitation, and so as to provide a more adequate habitat for modern life. (Such *aménagement* is already in practice in France.)

29 Social consequences of modern communication

We saw in Part Three that, as a result of the latest technology, and automation in particular, we were witnessing the start of a new and profound industrial revolution, as well as a social revolution affecting the tertiary occupations. Electronic computers are not the highly intelligent supermen whose mythology we have already referred to: computers cannot think, but they are aids to thought, and can carry out all the 'mechanical' and routine tasks connected with thinking much more efficiently than men, as well as all purely mechanical tasks in factories and offices.

This technological revolution has already begun to have repercussions on labour problems, by producing 'technological unemployment' of masses of workers, not skilled enough or too old to learn a type of work completely different from what they have been used to. Modern technology must of course free workers from the most mechanical tasks, just as earlier technological improvements freed them from the most physically arduous ones. Work will in future be much more a matter of thinking, planning, pressing buttons, moving little levers or other devices, and watching and controlling machines, than of what used to be called 'manual labour'. Manual jobs such as building, typewriting, book-keeping, office posts in general and various forms of handicrafts will be drastically reduced, and sooner or later eliminated altogether.

Extremely grave consequences will have to be faced, although Harold Wilson is the only politician of today who seems to have given serious thought to them. In general outline they are as follows:[101]

1) The uselessness of human energy, hitherto expended in work, but now to be replaced by the incomparably more speedy, economical and efficient electronic energy (atomic, and – in the distant future – solar and so on). 'Technological unemployment' is linked with this.

2) The short working day and probably also working period in every year, with longer free time and holidays. Work will thus not only occupy less time, but also be less monotonous and more humanised. Workers will not be slaves to their machines as hitherto, but make them work for them – or, better still, collaborate with them. The reverse of this picture is of course technological unemployment.

3) Automation will either lead to centralisation of development or else facilitate decentralisation (this is a crucial issue in discussions on the subject).

4) The structure of society as a whole will be profoundly changed. Types of work as well as salaries, sport and culture among the workers will be de-proleterianised and equalised. This *material* liberation could either become *moral* liberation or be diverted to consumption and amusements without spiritual value. It does not appear that automation will of its own accord alter the economic structure either of socialism or neo-capitalism. The USSR and the United States, each in their different way, seem able to absorb technological changes without changing the established economico-political order in their respective countries. Technology is neutral with regard to values and ethico-political decisions.

However, this last statement must be taken with a certain reserve, for there is no doubt that the development of automation involves more State intervention – as Harold Wilson has perspicaciously realised – and is therefore likely to conflict with neo-liberalism, at least in the critical phase of adaptation to the new technology. Even the *time* when automation is introduced must be carefully planned and regulated. An enormous sum must be set aside to indemnify all 'irredeemable' workers, incapable of being 'reconditioned' to the new sorts of jobs; from among these a force could be recruited to give aid on a massive scale to underdeveloped countries by doing semi-technical work needed there. At a later stage the State will have to intervene to prevent a collapse in prices, maintain purchasing power, increase the demand for consumer goods and keep up the standard of living of the numerous people whose capacity for work has entirely depreciated. Leisure time will have to be organised, not by compulsion but by direction, so that good use is made of it. Apart from the necessary hours of rest and amusement, this will involve orientation towards further training, so that some of the old-style workers may be again fitted for employment. Earlier retirement and compulsory education until the age of seventeen or eighteen will be necessary expedients.

As will be seen, apart from the emergency measures that are necessary for the transition period, a *new education* must be provided. As we saw in Part Three, pedagogic communication is the basis of all other forms. The new programme can be summed up in two watchwords: *technological education* and *continuous education.*

In the United States there already exist 200,000 electronic

computer programmers, and it is calculated that by 1970 500,000 will be needed. Simpler programming, simpler electronic 'language' and new models of the machines themselves will combine to facilitate their use. However it will be necessary to create a great many simple operative jobs. No special training is needed for the handling of the smaller types of electronic computer for domestic or routine office use. (In the United States there are practical courses for secondary school students and it is calculated that in the next twenty years more than two million university graduates will be occupied in jobs connected with automation). However, to exploit all the possibilities of computers,[102] and within a given statistical series 'ask' the machine all possible questions from different points of view and with multiple correlations, needs full co-operation – a real symbiosis – between man and machine. It is quite true that the machines can do nothing that has not been programmed in advance by man, but the relation between them and man is still changing. Workers in the factories of the past were in a sense the 'servants' of their machines; today the position is reversed and we are increasingly surrounded by mechanical 'slaves'. But electronic computers are destined to become 'colleagues' rather than servants or slaves of man. By being connected directly with the human brain[103] they will enable it to register information instantly, and (if it is in a foreign language) translate it simultaneously. They will be connected with a long-distance network of communications of the most diverse kinds. However they cannot yet think, and as Egmont Hiller has explained in *Sie versagt vor dem Un-*

vorhergesehenen,[104] they cannot deal with the unexpected. Man and machines thus have mutual need of one another.

This perfect connection between man and 'his' apparatus – only comparable, it seems to me, to that of the motorist who completely identifies himself with his car and its capacity for speed, acceleration and equilibrium – will create a *new type of worker*, as has already been suggested, and put an end to or reduce to a minimum the differences between 'employees' and 'workmen', as their functions tend to become more similar. And whereas in the past the greater part of the human race worked for the idle few, today the opposite is happening – or will happen soon: a minority, consisting of executives, scientists and technologists, will be constantly at work, organising, thinking and invention, while the masses will have more and more leisure time. As Gaston Berger said, in the present stage of civilisation what we lack are 'inventors', who will carry out basic research, translate scientific propositions into technical rules, and set in motion administrative, organising and social activities. It does not matter that the new type of human being is a much better technician than orator, nor that he needs less imagination, and imagination of a different kind, nor that the old division between 'science' and 'letters' is tending to disappear and the latter to be thought of as 'literary sciences'. After a rigorously pragmatical period, pure research is again coming into its own, and universities and independent laboratories carrying out theoretical experiments and testing hypotheses purely in the interests of science (even though sometimes financed by industry) have regained the highest prestige, now that 'practical' men are beginning to understand how dependent they are on theory and that without it there can be no progress even in the field of technology.

We are now witnessing what Margaret Mead calls an 'explosion of information', and the 'permanent revolution' produced by it in the technological sphere; the second of our two watchwords – *continuous education* – is relevant here. The adult of today suddenly finds he must adapt himself to the new types of work required of him. But even a youth born into the new society with its rhythm of scientific and technological progress, has to go on studying and preparing himself for change of occupation if he does not want to be left behind. His best ally will be improvement in educational techniques, based on advances in information itself – the contents of libraries and university teaching communicated electronically, portable television screens, teleschools (there are already more than a hundred exclusively educational television stations in the United States), magazines devoted to electronics, and so on. Increased free time every day will give a studious man constant opportunities to acquire this necessary 'technological culture'.[105]

Occupational mobility excludes the exaggerated tendency to specialisation that has been one of the features of recent scientific and technological culture. The young must be well grounded in those branches of knowledge that form a basis for others, so avoiding the stagnation of a fixed 'curriculum', too narrow specialisation, or jobs that are too limited and circumscribed. The worker of the immediate future needs a training that applies the chief branches of knowledge to his new occupation and provides a basis for the more specialised skills it demands,[106] while scientists will have to devote themselves more and more to studies linking together the different disciplines.

Those still full of energy for work, who yet feel incapable of being conditioned for new jobs by this form of 'continuous education', can escape from technological unemployment by working in underdeveloped countries. This would be an extension of the Peace Corps created by Kennedy, and an important contribution to international communication; it would probably develop slowly, starting with modest and limited objectives and progressing by degrees.[107]

There is no doubt that we are rapidly advancing towards a *new society*. The transition period will be hard, especially for the old, those who are 'set' in their ways, or naturally ill-equipped for the new, primarily audio-visual forms of understanding, in which acquisition of skills and extremely rapid reflexes are all-important. The sort of man best adapted to the new situation will have a new *attitude* to machines, treating them as collaborators as we have said. And this attitude, realistically and objectively formulated, will become a standard for general behaviour. Of course there will be difficulties to overcome, and the transition cannot therefore be left to chance or individual initiative but must be carefully planned so as to avoid too rapid change, loss of direction and serious economic and social dislocation.

I believe that we can look forward to the future of the machine age with calm confidence. Man can never be dominated by technology. Machines in themselves are not alarming. They merely increase man's power, as much for good as for evil. If at times the masses seem to be reduced to a huge army of automata, it is not the fault of the machines but of the men who control them, and the men who have allowed themselves to be controlled. Automation, like everything else affecting man's life, embodies both threats and promises. But it seems more reasonable to have faith in man and his inventions than to give way to pessimism. Supposing that automation contains a poison – and this is an exaggerated view, for it only contains a threat – we must not forget the lesson taught us by history, that every civilisation secretes both poison and antidote. Ethical decisions cannot be eliminated by automation; we ourselves would be responsible if we abandoned them, and this would be equivalent to renouncing our *human condition.* Man cannot be reduced to a collection of responses to a complex system of sign-stimuli. Perhaps some day the men of the future will see the present-day *revolution of information* as we regard such revolutions in the past as railways or Impressionist paintings: the one as a rather antiquated form of locomotion, the other as an attractive decoration for middle-class homes.

Notes and bibliography

1 *Language and Communication*, McGraw Hill, 1951.
2 *Mind, Self and Society*.
3 C.K. Ogden and I.A. Richards, *The meaning of meaning*.
4 The word 'symbol' immediately and inevitably evokes this 'mystical' relation.
5 Not merely the question of eliminating metaphysics, but of showing its essentially problematical character.
6 Karl Bühler, *Theory of Language*.
7 *Signs, Language and Behavior*, New York, 1946.
8 Cf. the beginning of the *Philosophical Investigations*, Blackwell, 1958. Also pp. 15–16, where he explains St Augustine's view of language as that of a child in a strange country whose language was unknown to him: in this situation the child can 'think' but not 'speak'. And 'think' would here mean something like 'talk to himself'.
9 Op. cit., p. 19.
10 On what follows cf. my preface to the anthology of the works of Unamuno, published by the Fondo de Cultura Económica, Mexico–Madrid.
11 Cf. Gaston Berger and Bertrand de Jouvenel, also T.J. Gordon and Olaf Helmer, *Report on a long-range forecasting study*, copyright of the Rand corporation, Santa Monica, California, 1964.
12 Shannon is the classic writer on the subject. Cf. Shannon, Warren Weaver, *The Mathematical Theory of Communication*, 1949. A lucid and accessible work by two Russians is A.M. and I.M. Jaglon's *Wahrscheinlichkeit und Information*. Cf. also *Symbols, signs and noise. Nature and process of communication*, by J.R. Pierce, a disciple of Shannon's.
13 A vocable with associations in ordinary language.
14 Apart from the classic work on this subject – *Theory of Games and Economic Behaviour* by von Neumann and Morgenstern – the following may be consulted: T.C. Schelling's *The Strategy of Conflict* and R.B. Braithwaite's *Theory of Games as a Tool of the Moral Philosopher*.

15 Cf. the author's 'La moral de Gracián', published in the *Revista de la Universidad de Madrid*, Vol. VII, No. 27, 1959, and in French in the *Revue de Metaphysique et de Morale*. In another work on 'Le Régime politique Espagnol en 1971' (SEDEIS, 'Futuribles' series, 10 July 1961), I have given other examples of concealed or essentially ambiguous strategy, especially with reference to the ambiguity of the relation between Francoism and the monarchy.

Understanding life as a game is perhaps a characteristic of those of us who prefer the game of life to games that 'distract' us from it. If I may be allowed a personal anecdote – when I recently had to go before an academic tribunal, I thought of it as a game; and without having recourse to 'dissimulation' or the rest of Gracián's artifices, but on the contrary by playing fairly and justifying my own actions, I tried to anticipate the intentions of my adversary (the new recruit to the law who played the judge) and disarm him – sometimes instinctively, so that he lost his head and exceeded his rights, reprehensibly in my view, at other times with calculation by exposing the series of connected expedients he was trying to pass off as individual ones. I found the game absorbing, until it was my turn to stop being ingenuous and realise that it was only 'the game of a game' – that it had been decided beforehand who should win and who lose, and that whatever happened the decision would be 'political' and have nothing to do with the way we played. From that moment I lost absolutely all interest in the contest, became indifferent to the result, and dedicated myself to more serious matters, such as writing this book.

16 On the relation between politics and ethics cf. *Ética y Política*, Ediciones Guadarrama, Madrid.

17 As is well-known, the word 'automation' was invented by John Diebold, of Harvard University, as a contraction of the word 'automatisation'. The contraction has been adopted in France, while in Germany it is called 'Automatisierung'. The

Royal Academy of the Spanish Language decided, probably rightly, that 'automatización' was linguistically preferable to 'automación'. But from the pedagogic point of view this decision has the grave disadvantage of obscuring the distinction between the old meaning of 'automático' as rigidly mechanical, and the new 'automación' or 'automatización'.

18 This has not prevented occasional hasty conclusions being reached in this field, as in others referring to human beings. My friend Gillo Dorfles's interesting, acute and well-informed book *Nuovi riti, nuovi miti*, Turin, 1965, quotes two other writers – Di Chapanis and Sapir. The first says: 'A couple of hundred years ago it was the vogue that man is nothing more than a system of complicated levers and pneumatic tubes (the nerves and blood vessels) which carry energising liquids. Fifteen or so years ago, it was popular to say that man is nothing but an information-handling channel. Call man a machine if you will, but do not underestimate him when you experiment on him. He is a non-linear machine, a machine which is programmed with a tape you cannot find . . .' (*Research Techniques in Human Engineering*.) The second: 'We respond to gestures with an extreme alertness and . . . in accordance with a secret code that is written nowhere'. (*Selected Writings*, published by Mandelbaum, University of California Press, 1951.)

19 The word 'significance' here correlated with 'sign' is equivocal and very inadequate. Might it be better to use Ogden and Richards' 'referent', or C.W. Morris's 'designatum'?

20 On this subject consult *The communication of emotional meaning*, by Joel Davitz *et alii*, McGraw Hill; it is also interesting about oral communication with special reference to inflexion, tone of voice, speed or slowness, etc. in the transmission of spoken language.

21 Cf. 'Para una teoria del talante', in the introduction to my book *Catolicismo y protestantismo como formas de existencia*, Editorial Revista de Occidente, Madrid.

22 *El Espectador*, III. (Cf. *Obras Completas*, vol. II, pp. 229 ff.)
23 Cf. *O.C.*, III, 353 ff.
24 On this subject see A. A. Moles, *Théorie de l'information et perception esthétique*, Paris, 1958.
25 On totemism see C. Lévi-Strauss, *Le totémisme aujourd'hui.*
26 *Philosophy in a new Key. A Study in the Symbolism of Reason, Rite and Art*, Chapter 6.
27 Op. cit., Chapter 7. Susanne Langer, a German by birth and a student at Vienna, has enriched the American school with the heritage of the great German thinkers. On myth – or myths – and their deep significance cf. P. Ricoeur, *Finitude et culpabilité*, especially vol. 2.
28 Obviously we cannot here consider the question of latent Christian myths or their destruction.
29 Cf. Wiener, *Cybernetics and Society*, wherein the author certainly gives way to exaggerated enthusiasm over the results of an extraordinary discovery (presented in his book *Cybernetics*, 1948); it does not, however, deserve the unfavourable judgement too hastily passed on it by H. Schelsky at the beginning of his title book *Die sozialen Folgen der Automatisierung*, Düsseldorf, 1957.
30 S. E. Toulmin, *The place of reason in ethics.*
31 Quoted by C. Lévi-Strauss in *Le totémisme aujourd'hui*, p. 138.
32 This 'tragoedia hominis moderni', as he calls it, has been well described in a recent book by Cornelio Fabro, *Introduzione all'ateismo moderno*, Editrice Studium, Roma, 1964.
33 *Concilium*, Revista Internacional de Teologia, No. 6.
34 See my contribution to *El amor y el erotismo*, Colección 'Tiempo de España' No. 3, Insula, Madrid, 1965, pp. 26–7.
35 *Preuves*, Paris, July 1965, pp. 12 ff.
36 M. Porebski, quoted by Dorfles, *Nuovi riti, nuovi miti*, p. 236.
37 *Mythologies*, 1957.
38 *L'esprit du temps*, 1962.
39 *Les structures anthropologiques de l'imaginaire*, 1963.

40 *Nuovi riti, nuovi miti*, 1965.

41 For a clear, brief account of this see G.A. Miller, *Language and communication*, chapter 12. For more detail cf. Robert F. Bales, *The Equilibrium Problem in Small Groups*, and T. Parsons, R.F. Baker and E.A. Shils, *Working Papers in the Theory of Action*, Free Press, 1953.

42 Between church and 'meetings' there is another natural channel of communication for macrogroups – the theatre, whose importance in ancient Greece, Shakespeare's England and Lope's Spain is obvious.

43 B.L. Smith, H.D. Lasswell and R.D. Casey, *Propaganda, Communication and Public Opinion*, 1946; also 'The Structure and Function of Communication in Society' in *The Communication of Ideas*, edited by L. Bryson, Institute for Religious and Social Studies, 1948.

44 Cf. D. Riesman and E.T. Riesman 'Movies and Audiences', in D. Riesman (ed.) *Individualism reconsidered*, The Free Press of Glencoe, 1964.

45 The Spanish Institute of Public Opinion published in 1964 a voluminous *Study of mass-communication media in Spain*; the first volume dealt with the press, the second with television, cinema, theatre and books. Technically fairly well done, its analyses of content were limited to comparisons between different classes and sections. As might be expected of an official publication, it was outstandingly innocuous and did not raise any interesting subjects and certainly not that of the development of 'content' during the twenty-five years of the Régime. However a few interesting facts emerge: the very low circulation of Spanish newspapers; the purely ideological character of the Fascist press, all its papers having incredibly low circulations and very little advertising space (the relation between the two is obvious); the exceptional situation of *Pueblo*, which does not really belong to the Movement but to the Syndicates, and which a thorough investigation would probably show to be the only Spanish daily paper people buy

(especially the young) not out of habit or because they must have some paper or other, but because they really want to read it; the paradoxical shortage of religious news in a 'Catholic State', and the equally paradoxical shortage of news about labour in a State which is constantly boasting of its social progress.

46 See, in Spanish, the 'Bibliografia anotada para un estudio de los contenidos de la televisión', by Jesús Garcia Jimenez, published in the *Revista de Educación*, January 1965.

47 W. Benjamin, *Das Kunstwerk im Zeitalter seiner technischen Reproduzierbarkeit*, Suhrkamp, Frankfurt, 1963, p. 48 ff.

48 Cf. *The human use of beings. Cybernetics and Society*.

49 WASP = White Anglo-Saxon Protestant.

50 The distinction between the two with respect to communication – language in general – has been gone into in Part One of this book, as the reader will remember.

51 'Les sciences humaines et le pouvoir', in *Esprit*, April 1965, p. 700. See also *The Social Function of Science*, London 1939, by J. D. Bernal, who has written much on the subject.

52 Among the copious literature on this subject the following may be consulted: 'The Communication of Information' by Herbert Coblaus, in *The Science of Science*, edited by M. Goldsmith and R. Mackay, Souvenir Press, London, 1964; 'Waiting for Mr. Know-it-all, or Scientific Tools we could have now', in *Physics Today*, February 1962, edited by K. Way, N. B. Gove and R. van Lieshour; and 'Dialectique de la régle et du Symbole', by P. R. Brygoo in *Preuves*, July 1965.

53 *Televisione, realtà sociale*, A. Mondadori, 1964.

54 Reyner Banham (quoted by G. Dorfles, op. cit., p. 195–6) has given this as the reason for the sensational success of the 'twist', whereas the 'madison' never caught on. The 'madison' was a revival of an old dance and therefore not acceptable today.

On this reciprocal influence and the self-selection by which the receptor selects what interests him and rejects the rest, see the excellent study by J. W. Riley Jr. and Matilda W. Riley, 'Mass Communication and the Social System', in *Sociology Today*, edited by Merton and others, and published under the auspices of the American Sociological Society by Basic Books Inc., New York, 1959, pp. 563–70 and 544–7.

55 On this subject cf. J. A. Culbertson and S. P. Hencley, *Educational Research: New Perspectives*, Danville, Illinois, 1963.

56 R. J. Havighurst and B. L. Neugarten. *Society and Education*, Boston, 1962, p. 126.

57 Cf. Robert Escarpit, *La révolution du livre*, Unesco et P.U.F., Paris, 1965.

58 Burton R. Clark, *Adult Education in Transition: A Study of Institutional Insecurity*, University of California, 1956.

59 Another more important and simpler manner of preserving non-communication between groups or social classes is by establishing private schools and colleges and free universities. Their higher fees and generally denominational character produce automatic segregation. Money and religious beliefs – so frequently and suspiciously found together – combine to exclude all but the upper classes from these centres of learning.

60 Cf. S. Ossowski, *Class structure in the social consciousness*, Routledge, London.

61 *Les Héritiers. Les Etudiants et le Culture*, Les Editions de Minuit, Paris, 1964. See also my review of this book in an article entitled 'Sociologia de la Educación en Francia y en España', published in the *Revista de Occidente*, June, 1965.

62 Cf. the volume edited by A. H. Halsey, Jean Floud and C. Arnold Anderson, *Education, Economy and Society*, The Free Press of Glencoe, 1961.

63 Cf. Harold L. Hodgkinson, *Education in Social and Cultural Perspectives*, 1962.

64 The reader will remember what was said about pure and applied science when speaking of scientific communication. A

doctrinaire State advocates a theory that is directly applicable to politics, and in many cases to the transformation of society, its economy and culture.

65 On the tension between administrative body, teaching staff and research teams in American universities cf. the book already referred to, *Educational Research: New Perspectives*; it also has a bearing on section 21 of the present work.

66 Ibid., p. 61.

67 Neal Gross, 'The Sociology of Education', in *Sociology Today*, edited by R.K.Merton, L.Broom and L.S.Cottrell Jr., Basic Books Inc., New York, 1959. For more detail, see p. 511 ff. of Havighurst, Neugarten, and Willard Waller, *The Sociology of Teaching*, Russell & Russell, New York, 1961, pp. 9–10.

68 On the teacher as key figure in the interaction between society, school and pupils, cf. Havighurst and Neugarten, op. cit., p. 507.

69 Cf. W.B.Brookover and D.Gottlieb, *A Sociology of Education*, American Book Company, 1964, and also W.Waller, op. cit., p. 279 ff., the chapter on 'Social distance; Buffer phrases'.

70 Cf. my essay *El Futuro de la Universidad*, Taurus Ediciones, Madrid. (Also published in German in the review *Frankfurter Hefte*.)

71 In *Rapports*, not yet published in book form. Cf. also their book already quoted.

72 Professor Stogdill tells us that, in reaction to the earlier situation when the social sciences were treated as a branch of philosophy, pragmatism became so dominant during the First World War that 'we began to think of ourselves as technicians not scientists'. (R.M.Stogdill, 'Role of Perception and Fulfilment in Research', in the collection *Educational Research* already referred to).

73 Cf. W.Waller, op. cit., pp. 49 ff.; he gives a vivid picture of the isolation of teachers, especially in small communities.

74 Cf. Bourdieu and Passeron, op. cit.

75 Cf. in *The Sociology of Education. A Source Book*, edited by R. R. Bell, The Dorsey Press, Homewood, Illinois, 1962, Bell's article, 'Decreasing Student and Community Identification with the School'.

76 Cf. the articles published by Ch. E. Bildwell and R. S. Vreeland (*Administrative Sciences Quarterly*, September 1963 and also in *The Sociological Quarterly*), on Education and Orientation.

77 Cf. the book quoted above, *Das Kunstwerk im Zeitalter seiner technischen Reproduzierbarkeit*.

78 Op. cit., p. 32.

79 G. Dorfles, op. cit., p. 168.

80 Not the same thing as sociology of art, at most a branch of it.

81 American sociology prefers to investigate social problems from the point of view of *individual status* or *social stratum* rather than *class*, and raises the question of 'communication' in connection with the different attributes defining status or membership of a stratum: profession, income, culture, race, social origin, part of the town lived in and standard of life in general. But obviously we cannot here go into the question of congruity or incongruity – communication or non-communication to use the terminology we have adopted here – between these 'advantages' or signs of social position.

82 This last point is dealt with in my article in number two of *Euros*, a European review with editions in English, French, German, Spanish and Dutch.

83 Including publicity research. In Spain, for example, the Institute of Public Opinion, as it is called, is dependent on the Ministry of Information (= Propaganda).

84 *Introduction à la Politique*, N.R.F., p. 222.

85 Op. cit., p. 228. A reasonably critical Marxist would not, I think, find it difficult to accept this conclusion of Duverger's. The important thing about a system is its structure, not the psychological intentions of those who collaborate in it.

86 With reference to what follows see my article 'Openness to the World: an Approach to World Peace', published in the Harvard review *Daedalus*, for December 1965.

87 For examples of both see Felix Greene's *A Curtain of Ignorance*. (*How the American Public has been misinformed about China*), Doubleday, 1964; and my article 'La imagen española de Alemania', first published in the German review *Dokumente*, No. 1, 1 February 1957, and later in my book *La juventud europea y otros ensayos*, Seix Barral, 1962.

88 Among these, see the work of T. J. Gordon and O. Helmer, already quoted, *Report on a long-range forecasting study* and its bibliography. The English review *New Scientist* is also very interesting.

89 Georges Bastide, *Traité de l'action morale*, pp. 83–4.

90 Quoted by Bertrand de Jouvenel, 'De la Conjecture', 'Futuribles', 20 March 1962.

91 Jouvenel, loc. cit., and Daniel Bell, 'Douze modes de prévision en science sociale', 'Futuribles', 20 September 1963.

92 Jouvenel, 'Recherches sur la décision', 'Futuribles', 20 January 1962; G. L. Shackle, *Decision, Order and Time in Human Affairs*, 1961, and G. T. Guilbaud *et alii*, *La Décision*, 1961.

93 *L'Homme moderne et son Éducation*, P.U.F., 1962.

94 T. A. Sumberg, 'The more abundant life', in *The American Journal of Economics and Sociology*, January 1962. Professor Tierno has maintained a similar position.

95 Friedrich Pollock, *Automation*, Frankfurt, 1956.

96 Why is there no Spanish word for this? The Italians have invented the word 'fantascienza', and also 'fumetti' for 'comics', which we Spaniards call 'tebeos', thus spreading the false notion that this fundamentally visual medium of communication is meant solely for children. But in this, as in other things, modern adults are much like children.

97 Cf. P. Bourdieu and others, *Un art moyen. Essai sur les usages sociaux de la photographie*, Les Editions de Minuit, Paris, 1965.

98 Another word that has no exact equivalent in Spanish, probably because the *tempo* of our activity is slower and we therefore make do with our night's sleep and the sensible tradition of the 'siesta'.

99 Cf. for example Jacques Ellul, 'L'homme occidental en 1970', 'Futuribles', 10 November 1961.

100 In the Anglo-Saxon countries the sociology of law, unlike its totalitarian counterpart directly or indirectly inspired by Marxism, tends to be analytical and deal with problems like the relation of sociological jurisprudence to abstract legality, the role and social status of judges and barristers, juries as representatives of society, custom and law, common law and society, and so on. From the point of view adopted in the present book, it is interesting that P. Selznick emphasises the function of 'two-way communication' between sociology and law. (Cf. his article, 'The Sociology of Law', in the volume *Sociology Today*, by Merton and others, already quoted.)

101 Cf. H. Schelsky, *Die sozialen Folgen der Automatisierung*, Eugen Diederichs Verlag, Düsseldorf-Cologne, 1957, p. 25, and Egmont Hiller, *Automaten und Menschen*, Deutsche Verlag-Anstalt, Stuttgart, 1958, pp. 77 ff.

102 Another word that has no exact equivalent in Spanish.

103 T. J. Gordon and O. Helmer, op. cit., pp. 43 and 41–2.

104 Op. cit., p. 90.

105 Cf. J. W. Powell, *Channels of Learning: The story of Educational Television*, Washington, 1962. The following example from the very recent past, quoted by Gaston Berger, illustrates the relation of constant scientific change to 'continuous education': 'Imagine a sixty-year-old doctor who knows nothing beside what he learned in medical school as a student: he would not have heard of sulphanilamides, antibiotics, cardiac surgery, radio-isotopes, nor a hundred other means of diagnosis or therapy. It is obvious that no doctor can exist throughout his career on what he learned at the start of it.

The same is true of many other professions.' (*L'Homme moderne et son Education*, p. 119.) It will soon be possible to say outright that this happens in *every* profession. The 'class' distinctions in the purely technological society of the future will lie between those who keep permanently informed and those who fall behind.

106 Cf. L. H. Evans, G. E. Arnstein *et alii*, *Automation and the Challenge to Education*, Washington, 1962.

107 Frederick Schuman, *The Commonwealth of Man*, New York, 1952.

Acknowledgments

Acknowledgment is due to the following for illustrations (the number refers to the page on which the illustration appears): Frontispiece and 108 The Direction Generale du tourisme; 13 Tony Ciolkowski; 14, 17, 130, 149, 163, 179 and 219 The United States Information Service; 16, 31, 101, 104–5, 116 and 221 Camera Press; 20 Magnum Photos; 21 Associated Newspapers; 22 and 150 The Postmaster General; 23 The Royal National Institute for the Blind; 55 The British Film Institute; 56–7 The National Film Archive and Associated British Pathe; 59 Mr Colin Haycraft; 60 The Warburg Institute; 71 Universal Edition, Vienna; 74 SPADEM and The Tate Gallery; 77 University of Nebraska Art Galleries, Lincoln, Neb.; 99 Novosti Press Agency; 101 Paul Popper Photo; 106 and 117 Keystone Press Agency Ltd; 107 The Nationalbibliothek, Vienna; 113 The Mansell Collection; 120 Syndication International; 123 Francoise Foliot; 129, 166 and 167 Radio Times Hulton Picture Library; 148 International Business Machines Ltd; 160 The Church Missionary Society; 182 Messrs Guinness Ltd; 183 Brinylon Ltd; 185 The Stedelijk Museum, Amsterdam; 186–7 The Tate Gallery; 223 Aerofilms Ltd.

Index

Philosophy and Religion

Christianity
W. O. Chadwick, *Cambridge*

Monasticism
David Knowles, *London*

Judaism
J. Soetendorp, *Amsterdam*

The Modern Papacy
K. O. von Aretin, *Göttingen*

Witchcraft
Lucy Mair, *London*

Sects
Bryan Wilson, *Oxford*

Language and Literature

A Model of Language
E. M. Uhlenbeck, *Leyden*

French Literature
Raymond Picard, *Paris*

Russian Writers and Society 1825–1904
Ronald Hingley, *Oxford*

Satire
Matthew Hodgart, *Sussex*

The Romantic Century
Robert Baldick, *Oxford*

The Arts

The Language of Modern Art
Ulf Linde, *Stockholm*

Architecture since 1945
Bruno Zevi, *Rome*

Twentieth Century Music
H. H. Stuckenschmidt, *Berlin*

Aesthetic Theories since 1850
J. F. Revel, *Paris*

Art Nouveau
S. Tschudi Madsen, *Oslo*

Academic Painting
Gerald Ackerman, *Stanford*

Palaeolithic Cave Art
P. J. Ucko and A. Rosenfeld, *London*

Primitive Art
Eike Haberland, *Mainz*

Romanesque Art
Carlos Cid Priego, *Madrid*

Expressionism
John Willett, *London*

Psychology and Human Biology

The Molecules of Life
Gisela Nass, *Munich*

The Variety of Man
J. P. Garlick, *London*

Eye and Brain
R. L. Gregory, *Cambridge*

The Ear and the Brain
E. C. Carterette, *U.C.L.A.*

The Biology of Work
O. G. Edholm, *London*

The Psychology of Attention
Anne Treisman, *Oxford*

Psychoses
H. J. Bochnik, *Hamburg*

Psychosomatic Medicine
A. Mitscherlich, *Heidelberg*

Child Development
Phillipe Muller, *Neuchâtel*

Man and Disease
Gernot Rath, *Göttingen*